A COUNSELOR'S INTRODUCTION TO NEUROSCIENCE

A Counselor's Introduction to Neuroscience is a guidebook to neuro-biology that is customized for counselors' unique goals and requirements. Drawing on years of experience, not only in the lab but in the counselor's chair, the authors unravel the complexities of neuroscience and present an easily understood volume that is an essential companion for any counselor who wishes to expand his or her understanding of the human brain, how it works, and how it creates our identities.

Bill McHenry, PhD, is the coauthor of *A Contemporary Approach to Substance Abuse and Addiction Counseling* and *What Therapists Say and Why They Say It*.

Angela M. Sikorski, PhD, is an associate professor of psychology at Texas A&M University-Texarkana.

Jim McHenry, EdD, is professor emeritus of counseling and human development at Edinboro University of Pennsylvania and the coauthor of *What Therapists Say and Why They Say It*.

A COUNSELOR'S INTRODUCTION TO NEUROSCIENCE

Bill McHenry, Angela M. Sikorski, and Jim McHenry

Routledge
Taylor & Francis Group

NEW YORK AND LONDON

First published 2014
by Routledge
711 Third Avenue, New York, NY 10017

and by Routledge
27 Church Road, Hove, East Sussex BN3 2FA

Routledge is an imprint of the Taylor & Francis Group, an informa business

Library of Congress Cataloging-in-Publication Data

McHenry, Bill, 1971–
A counselor's introduction to neuroscience / Bill McHenry, Angela M.
   Sikorski, and Jim McHenry.
      pages cm
   Includes bibliographical references and index.
   1. Neuropsychology.   2. Neurobiology.   3. Counseling.
   I. Sikorski, Angela M.   II. McHenry, Jim, 1937–   III. Title.
QP360.M3535   2013
612.8—dc23   2013009300

ISBN: 978-0-415-66227-7 (hbk)
ISBN: 978-0-415-66228-4 (pbk)
ISBN: 978-0-203-07249-3 (ebk)

Typeset in Baskerville
by Apex CoVantage, LLC

Printed and bound in the United States of America
By Edwards Brothers Malloy on sustainably paper

This book is dedicated to the mental health professionals who serve the various and varied needs of their clients, to the clients who deserve the very best care our field can offer, and to the authors, researchers, and professionals whose prior efforts served as wonderful guides to our work.

CONTENTS

TABLES, FIGURES, AND CASES

Cases

ABOUT THE AUTHORS

Dr. Angela Sikorski is an associate professor of psychology at Texas A&M University–Texarkana who studies experience-induced brain plasticity and the neurobiology of learning and memory. After completing her PhD in experimental psychology from the University of Wisconsin–Milwaukee, she was a postdoctoral fellow in the biology department at the University of Texas–San Antonio. In her spare time, Dr. Sikorski enjoys playing tennis, knitting, and spending time on Shawano Lake with her family. Despite her current residence, she is—and always will be—a devout Packer fan.

Dr. Bill McHenry is an associate professor of counseling and psychology at Texas A&M University-Texarkana. He has been a counselor educator for the last decade. Bill worked as a counselor in numerous diverse settings that include schools, universities, agencies, mental health centers, and rehabilitation programs. He has coauthored three other books and numerous professional journal articles. He enjoys family time, fishing, and losing to his wife at Ping-Pong.

Dr. Jim McHenry was a professor at Edinboro University of Pennsylvania for 32 years and is now a semiretired professor emeritus.

In addition to his campus teaching duties, he also served as co-ordinator of the Rehabilitation Counseling Program, director of the campus program for disadvantaged students, and counselor for students with disabilities. He has coauthored two other books and numerous professional journal articles. He carries a 12 handicap in golf (nine holes).

CONTRIBUTORS

Special contributions to this book were made by several uniquely qualified and talented individuals.

Dr. Tommie Hughes, associate professor of psychology at Texas A&M University-Texarkana, contributed much needed information, data, and clarity to chapter 7, Assessment of Brain Function.

As a significant part of the offerings in this book, the following images were created by two artists:

Ms. Alexandra Faith Walker contributed ten images to this book that show readers what words alone cannot convey (Figures P.1, 2.1, 2.2, 2.3, 2.4, 2.5, 4.1, 5.5, 6.1, and 7.2).

Dr. Angela Sikorski Figures 3.1, 3.4, and 3.5

PREFACE

You may or may not recognize the model below (Figure P.1), but there was a time, from 1810 until about the 1840s, when it represented a widely accepted explanation of how the human brain actually functioned. The practice, *phrenology,* was formulated by Franz Joseph Gall, a German physician. Gall held that the human brain was made up of 27 *organs* whose relative size could be measured by the fingertips and palms of trained phrenologists. Today, of course, phrenology is widely recognized as bosh and hogwash, as *pseudo* science. Nevertheless, Gall did contribute to the advancement of brain studies by suggesting that thoughts and emotions were housed in separate parts of the brain. So let us credit Gall with at least one correct hunch while we relegate his model to the mantel as a curiosity and move on.

Alas, even as we rid ourselves of that porcelain model depicting Galls' model a century-and-a-half later, we are left with few absolutes regarding the brain. Still, we can in fact cite one. You are actually using it right now as you read these words. It is perched right there between your ears, roughly located above your neck and shoulders, snugly nestled within your skull. *Your* brain is the most complex planetary entity known to man. *Absolutely.* Words like incredible, wonderful, stupendous, amazing, and the like truly pale as accolades.

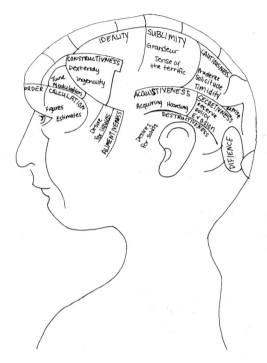

Figure P.1 **A model of phrenology**

So, once we quit poking fun at Gall's efforts and prior to look-ing at some actual and very significant findings neurologists have made to date, a bit of humility may be in order. From that posi-tion, let us allow that this book is an ambitious effort intended to show how some of the incredibly important research now being done on the human brain can be effectively utilized by counsel-ing practitioners in their day-to-day work with real, live hurting clients.

This is certainly a daunting task. The brain has been pon-dered, prodded, sliced, and diced probably from the beginning of humankind. As noted above, many of those early efforts were misguided: many, totally off the mark. Today, however, with the development of technological marvels such as MRIs, fMRIs, CATs, PETs, and the like, skilled researchers are beginning to unlock secrets heretofore either totally unknown or only guessed at. As those findings continue to emerge, of course, the potential they present to those working in the helping professions is almost beyond measure. Such potential presents itself in a number of ways.

Certainly, as we gain more understanding of the chemistry of the brain, we increase the potential effectiveness of pharmacological interventions. This is significant for counselors since a combination of the two—pharmacology and counseling—has generally been found to be more effective in producing positive outcomes than the use of either intervention alone. Naturally, as with much in life, the devil is in the details. What kinds and how much medication? What kind of counseling?

So we—neurologists, pharmacists, counselors, and patients/clients—all face large challenges. But, through the use of truly amazing technological advances that allow us to glimpse the workings of the brain in ways never before available in history, we now have more tools than ever before.

Further, as counselors know, regardless of what we come to learn about the brain, there are still immeasurable aspects to the counseling process that stand as either obstacles or resources for clients wrestling with their psychological problems, namely free will, the human spirit, and, of course, willingness to change.

Additionally, and perhaps in the same voice of reason, we find that there really are two entities that reside within the hardened fortress of the skull: the brain and the mind. Although some may consider the two to be similar, or even the same entity, we start this book with that premise and promise to you as readers that we see vast differences in what we consider the brain (and its many components and interconnections, billions of neurons and trillions of connections wired together in ways that we still cannot fully grasp) versus the mind of the individual client, which, in addition to carrying the physical properties of the brain, is even more indefinable. Words like "faculty of consciousness," "ability to reason and remember," "attention," and "will" come to *mind* (or is it *brain?*). Somewhere, within this pair (or in both) are the memories, lived life experiences, ways of knowing and transacting with the world, and rhythms of everyday lifestyle that are completely unique to the particular individual. Therefore, even as we attempt to understand these formidable entities, we agree with Kay (2009):

> Neurons do not define the essence of people, nor do deficiencies in neurotransmitters explain mental disorders. (p. 288)

However, while recognizing Kay's caution, our efforts *are* centered on the entity known as the human brain. We also note at the onset that the knowledge contained and described in this book, while meant to aid in counseling with clients, is not designed to systematically define exact treatment protocols for clients suffering from, for example, _____ (fill in the blank with an issue or mental health disorder).

Yet another author captures our view of the brain and perhaps the awe with which we approach this subject. As others have suggested before us—and paradoxically (because without the brainpower our species has developed over time, we could not explore our brains in the first place)—perhaps the most complex thing in the universe is that thing that we seek to explore the most: the human brain.

We would like to say one word about how we wrote this book. We have made every effort to present current and useful information that informs counselors about the great opportunities available through better understanding neuroscience and its relation to the field of counseling. In doing so, we have had to rely, at times, on some heavy doses of neuro-based language. Because we are operating under the assumption that most counselors or counselors-in-training are not fully versed in such language, we have tried to present this new language in small doses. We hope the book is both informative and user friendly for you as a counselor.

The layout of our book represents the continuum of knowledge and utility of brain function and the counseling process. In chapter 2, *Overview of the Brain and Central Nervous System,* we introduce basic neuroscience language as well as initiate the process of helping you recognize the overlap between neurobiology and counseling. This chapter also contains a thorough description of the brain and CNS (central nervous system). We have tried not to delve too deeply into the neuro-language and attempted to minimize technical jargon as much as possible. Because the primary goal for this chapter is to help you anchor each of the major aspects to brain function within the actual process of counseling.

In chapter 3, *Brain Development and Brain Plasticity,* we continue the process of discussing brain function, in this case from a developmental perspective. Because counselors frequently work with clients across the spectrum of life, we would be quite remiss if we did not introduce and discuss the major aspects of brain development at different stages of life. Again, we utilize the process of neuro-language using actual case examples of counseling process.

In chapter 4, *The Differential Impact of Different Counseling Approaches on the Brain,* we highlight the fact that when working with an individual client, the processes and procedures used by the counselor to elicit responses and help the client work through issues *are,* in fact, directly aligned with brain function (whether the counselor is aware of the processes or not). To help counselors make informed decisions about practice, we tie specific brain function with major aspects of major counseling theories. In essence, what parts of the brain are triggered, tripped, or caused to fire by using what type of approach by the counselor?

Moving into chapter 5, *Neurobiological, Neuropsychological Aspects of Mental Health,* we delineate and describe information for clinicians regarding neuro-function and mental health issues. In this chapter, we also consider both diagnosable and nondiagnosable issues as they relate to and pertain to brain function.

Following the emphasis on mental health issues and brain function, chapter 6, *Psychotropic Medications*, provides significant and substantial information for counselors to better understand not only what medications are commonly used with what disorders, but the actual impacts that these medications may have on brain function.

Chapter 7, *Assessment of Brain Function*, delineates certain processes of assessment of brain function within the client. This chapter allows counselors to better understand and possibly even utilize tools and techniques associated with brain function analysis. We cover the spectrum in this chapter, including tips and techniques used in the session to assess which parts of the brain are being predominantly used by the client; formal assessments; results; and how to incorporate and use such data in the clinical process.

In our final chapter, chapter 8, *Brain Activity in Action*, we attempt to pull it all together. We use language and concepts previously addressed in chapters 1–7 to highlight and annotate different parts of varied counseling sessions. Specific attention is paid to the responses of the client, as well as which parts of the brain are active during that part of each session. In addition, we look at how the counselor might purposefully and professionally call into play other regions of the brain in order to become even more effective and purposeful in the counseling process.

We hope you find the material that follows useful in your work with the clients you serve.

ACKNOWLEDGMENTS

First and foremost, I (Angie) would like to thank my husband, Jeff, and children, Michael and Noah, for supporting me throughout this project. I know having a wife and mother locked away in an office for hours on end was not always easy on you, and I sincerely thank you for your patience. I love you dearly and hope you will be as proud of this book as I am. I would also like to thank my parents, Jim and Dawn Parmentier, who have been my biggest cheerleaders since day one. There are no words to express how appreciative and grateful I am for everything you have done for me. Also, a special thank you to one of our most amazing graduate students, Katie Price, who without a single complaint was willing to drop everything at a moment's notice to help us with odds and ends. Last but not least, I would like to acknowledge my coauthors. This book would not be possible without you. This has been an amazing experience for me, and I look forward to many more collaborations together.

I (Bill) would like to sincerely thank my coauthors, Angie and Dad. This project has taken shape and form just as we discussed not so long ago. It has been a pleasure to work with you both and learn from your keen insight and deep understanding of the human brain and human psychology. Although this project is complete, I sense we have many more to accomplish together.

I very much want to thank our editorial team, especially Anna. Since our very first interaction, we have felt your positive energy toward our project and certainly realized your wonderful way of working with authors on helping them turn words and ideas into a book. Your guidance and advice had a significant positive impact on the book. I want to thank Ms. Katie Price for her efforts in helping us find meaningful and useful literature, research, and images for this book. Finally, I want to thank my wife Missy and children Meghan, Billy, Katie, and Shane for allowing me the time and serenity to complete this book.

I (Jim) wish to thank a number of people. First, I wish to thank my coauthors, son Bill (who ropes me in on these efforts) and certainly Angie (who has done some very, very fine work here). Also significant for me are grandsons Nick (working on his master's at Mercyhurst University), Jake (now an Edinboro University sophomore), and Alexa (a freshman—at Texas A&M–Texarkana, no less). They and Ryan and Ian, also grandsons, help me stay alert, as does the quartet of blessings Bill noted above. They really do keep me (somewhat) young, as do my daughters, Lisa (the entrepreneur) and Linda (a professor in her own right). The help I always get from my wife of 51 years, of course, usually goes without saying and after that many years, unfortunately, too often gets taken for granted. Thanks, honey. And finally, two others. My mother, Charlotte, who, if she were still alive, would be so proud of Bill and me (especially, of course, Bill!), and Dr. Wesley Hakanen, who got lost in the edits of one of our earlier books. Thanks, Wes.

GUIDE TO NEUROCOUNSELING LANGUAGE

Table 00 **Guide to Neurocounseling Language**

Neurons	Basic cells in the brain that receive, transmit, and integrate information
Glia	Non-neuronal supportive cells within the CNS
Central Nervous System	Part of the nervous system that includes the brain and spinal cord
Peripheral Nervous System	All other parts of the nervous system other than the brain and spinal cord (e.g., nerves in the hand)
Left Hemisphere	Part of the brain focused on writing, language, math, and logic
Right Hemisphere	Part of the brain focused on creativity, imagination, and music
Corpus Callosum	A collection of axons that travel from one hemisphere to another to enable cross-hemisphere communication
Axons	The part of the neuron that initiates and transmits the neural signal toward other cells
Gyrus	Bumps on the brain created to allow for increased brain size within the skull
Sulci	Minor grooves between the gyrus

(*Continued*)

Table 00 (*Continued*)

Fissures	Major grooves between the gyrus that denote/mark boundaries between hemispheres and lobes
Occipital Lobe	Part of the brain associated with visual perception and dreams
Temporal Lobe	Part of the brain associated with speech, memory, and emotion
Frontal Lobe	Part of the brain associated with reasoning and logic
Parietal Lobe	Part of the brain associated with information related to sensing stimuli and producing motor behavior
Cerebellum	Part of the brain associated with motor coordination
Myelin Sheath	Fatty layer of cells that cover the axons and help to speed up the dissemination of information
Dendrites	The part of the neuron that receives information from neighboring cells
Cell Body	The part of the neuron that integrates neural signals
Neurotransmitters	Chemicals made by the neuron to transmit information
Excitatory Neurotransmitters	Electrically charged to excite neighboring cells
Inhibitory Neurotransmitters	Electrically charged to inhibit information being shared by neighboring cells

1

AN INTRODUCTION TO THE INTERTWINED NATURE OF THE FIELDS OF NEUROBIOLOGY AND COUNSELING

Introduction

When we step back from the field of counseling for a moment and look from a distance, there are four major forces that have emerged in the last hundred or so years, each offering useful additions to practitioners' understanding of both clients and the counseling process. At present, we are poised on the cusp of yet another major breakthrough holding immense promise for helping us work even more effectively and purposefully with our clients. That fifth force combines the unfolding discoveries being garnered by combining neuroscientific information and the counseling process. That fifth force in counseling—neurocounseling—may, in fact, be upon us.

Of course, for this paradigm transition to take shape, our field must go through a metamorphosis. And, as we all are aware, change does not come easily. Consider, for example, working with a client who is stuck in a position of not wanting to meet or connect with other people. A skilled counselor can help the client see the worth and utility of engaging with others and perhaps even help the client take some small steps toward becoming more socially interested. Ultimately, however, it is entirely up to the client to actually make the decision to change his or her behavior and commit to modifying his/her behavior pattern. Sometimes such changes occur slowly over time. Such was the case in our field with the arrival of concepts like multicultural counseling and counseling diverse populations. Initially, for many counselor education programs, these issues were often completely "housed" in one course. And while for some time, many of the concepts needed to be an effective multicultural counselor did not grow roots beyond the "multicultural class," today in many counseling programs, real change has occurred and the connections between multicultural counseling and "other" counseling courses (e.g., Human Growth and Development, Assessment Techniques in Counseling, etc.) are clearly integrated within and across the curriculum—a curriculum, incidentally, which should be ideally seen as a dynamic, modifiable, changing, and developing system, not simply as a set of principles set in stone. Change occurs and positive changes usually do result in positive outcomes. We hope that the field agrees with us and the other authors espousing the value of understanding neurocounseling as a means to better working with clients. And we hope such inclusion in core curriculums occurs sooner rather than later.

For the practicing counselor, faced with the challenges of the unique needs of individual clients, continually enhancing your skill set simply makes both professional and pragmatic sense. In a like manner then—through experience, insight, environmental interaction, and growth and development itself—both the field of counseling and the human brain reap benefits.

So, we start this volume with a brief look at the changes that have occurred in counseling over the many years. We hope that it will become apparent to you that much of what you are now doing in your counseling practice does in fact have a positive impact on the restructuring and chemical composition of your clients' brains, and we hope that by further extending your knowledge base you will become even more effective and better able to meet your clients' neurological needs.

The First Force—Psychoanalysis

Sigmund Freud, pioneer of the field of psychoanalysis, is considered to be one of the most prominent voices in the field of counseling (Murdock, 2012). His theory and conjecture, lexicon and language, and approach to working with clients still permeate our work today (Goldschmidt & Roelke, 2012). Not just in the discipline of psychoanalysis, but also in many of the major theories of counseling, we can find artifacts and remnants of what Freud offered through his celebrated and controversial career (Murdock, 2012). Perhaps one of the most easily identified contributions of Freud's work to the current field of counseling was his use of the therapeutic conversation or "talking cure." Counseling is still anchored clearly and directly to the idea that through conversations that target specific psychological principles and approaches, clients can get better. People sometimes can get significantly better through the process of a healing therapeutic conversation (McHenry & McHenry, 2006). A review of the current information regarding neurocounseling demonstrates that there are distinct, measurable changes in the brain that can and do occur as a result of effective counseling sessions. People do not just feel better or change old patterns of thinking/behaving but actually modify their brain structure. Here we draw a parallel between counseling and learning.

Learning is often defined as a change in behavior due to experience (Chance, 2009), and there is a plethora of evidence to suggest that experience in and of itself leads to neural changes (Black et al., 1990; van Praag, Kempermann, & Gage, 1999b). Thus, the counseling experience can promote neuroplasticity and result in new/changed behavior (e.g., more effective coping). What follows is only one example of how counseling can impact actual brain structure. Do not be discouraged by the language (if you are unfamiliar); we will cover all of this in later chapters.

Kay (2009) identified three major metabolic changes related to the condition of a major depressive disorder (MDD). These three major differences between normally functioning brains and those of clients with MDD are (1) decreased activity in the prefrontal cortex (suggesting poor concentration and cognitive disturbances), (2) increased activity in the ventral brain structures (hypothesized to be connected to the presence of negative thinking), and (3) decreased activity in the basal ganglia (which may be associated with less reward of dopamine). Now, recall that Freud clearly suggested that through guided and purposeful dialog about problems, clients could get better, and the field of counseling has carried that torch for over a century without definitive proof. Today however, results of studies such as those conducted by Goldapple et al. (2004) and Kennedy et al. (2007) support the power and capability of clients' brains to actually change as a result of therapeutic conversations. Their research (using positive emission tomography [PET]) suggested that changes in the brain, and specifically in the regions identified as being part of the depressive disorder, changed for the better. In addition, Martin et al. (2001) found (using a single proton emission computerized tomography [SPECT]) that while both medications and psychotherapy provided positive changes in the basal ganglia, it was only the psychotherapy that resulted in positive changes in the limbic system.

Though these are just a few examples of the many studies we will discuss in this book, it should be clear from the outset that the technology now exists to test Freud's original theory of a talking cure, and in fact researchers are finding that he and the many, many counselors who have followed were/are on the right track.

Freud also provided us with another major and historic concept of the interpsychic forces of the id, ego, and superego. For Freud, the id was for the part of the person or personality that housed the drive to seek pleasure and avoid pain. He further added that it was through the id that our senses developed strong urges and desires toward things we most wanted. Unorganized and unstructured, the id needed something to help balance its insatiable appetite for pleasure. The ego provides the necessary structure for the id. Through the ego, the individual mind suppresses urges that are not acceptable within the environment. And, the superego, according to Freud, was the individual's sense of perfection and idealized version of self (Murdock, 2012).

Of course, this theory places a lot of emphasis on the pushes and pulls that occur intrapsychically within each of us. Regardless of the fact that to date neurological specialists have yet to find these parts of the brain (because they really do not physically exist in the basic biology of the brain), Freud's theory of these three major entities and the psychic forces that push and pull within each individual offers us a useful *metaphor* to help talk about, at least at the start of this book, the potential utility of understanding the brain more fully and how each of the various functions (chemicals, structure, elements, etc.) work as a gestalt rather than as unique and individual parts that are separated from and unrelated to one another.

In addition, this metaphor of the id, ego, and superego, as Freud suggested, was a necessary balancing act among the three. According to Freud, major failures in this balancing act were what led to mental illness. Conversely, in healthy brains, there is symmetry with all the interconnected and interdependent facets of the brain functioning in concert with one another. Failure for neural connections, elevated or diminished levels of necessary chemicals, and/or poor function within individual parts of the brain then can, and often do, cause clients to experience mental health concerns and issues. After Freud, the field of counseling was offered a second major force: behaviorism.

The Second Force—Behaviorism

It took two major theorists and many research-based examples of behavioral modification and change to help the field of counseling recognize the value and importance of incorporating behavioral change remedies into counseling practice. Primary behavioral theorists were John Watson and B. F. Skinner (Corey, 2009). Through systematic trials, behavioral research demonstrated that behavior could be altered through environmental manipulation techniques. Further, in addition to being demonstratively effective in changing the behavior of clients, when combined with cognitive approaches, such efforts helped clients modify their view of both self and others (Kay, 2009). Absent the advent or use of MRI machines, functional MRIs, or CAT scans, behaviorism grew in popularity through simply observing that people really can change when offered the right set of modifiers. Today, the field of neurocounseling has the ability to observe why these changes are possible and, in many cases, document actual physical changes in the brain as a result of behavioral modifiers (Linden, 2006).

For example, from a behavioral perspective, repeated traumatic experiences can lead to structural and systemic changes in the brain (Creeden, 2009; van der Kolk, 2003; Bremner, 2002; Perry, 2001). If you recall the concept of "conditioned responses" such as those used with Pavlov's dog, it is not a far stretch to consider that people who have been repeatedly traumatized over a period of years will exhibit conditioned responses to stimuli (e.g., loud noises). However, neurocounseling can benefit from the understanding that those responses are typically paired with internal changes in the brain and its overall structural response to environmental cues. Such physical changes within the brain may include limbic irritability, persistent increased activity in the amygdala, decreased hippocampal volume, and deficient left hemisphere development. In essence, negative behavioral training, such as in the case of repeated traumatic events, can have a negative physical change on the brain of a child or adult. Consequently, using a neurocounseling perspective, a counselor may target specific parts of the brain (identified above) through purposeful techniques to aid in the "healing" or positive restructuring of the client's brain.

The Third Force—Humanism

Carl Rogers and others ushered in a new direction for counseling when the approach to counseling called humanism was developed. Through multiple sources—Rollo May, Carl Rogers, Viktor Frankl, and Abraham Maslow (Gladding, 2001)—the identity of the humanistic perspective emerged. In essence, the keys to working with clients included Rogers' (1951) necessary and sufficient conditions for change (empathy, unconditional positive regard, and congruence), along with other therapeutic factors offered, such as respecting and utilizing the human spirit and helping clients make meaning from life rather than prescribing or directing their thinking (as was common in psychoanalytic approaches). And in response to the behaviorist model of creating change from external sources (modifiers of behavior), the humanists approached the counseling process as being facilitators of growth by the client from within (utilizing the clients existing resource) (Kay, 2009). Humanism taught the field that a talking cure, or therapeutic approach, can be effective not just from a one-up (medical model of practitioner knows what is best for the client) but also from more of a counselor as guide and facilitator of the client being the expert in their own life direction (Corey, 2009). This focus represented a major shift in the field of counseling.

While the intrinsic values of such approaches were being suggested by clinicians using a humanistic approach, there was no absolute data on what might be happening within the client's brain. Now, as the field of neurocounseling becomes more prominent in our literature, we have begun to understand more fully what really happens for some clients when such an approach is utilized.

Humanism essentially centers on the individual's search for meaning, incorporating in that search the intrinsic motivation driving him or her toward a new way of being in and with the world. This focus holds that by coupling self-drive and self-regulation with new understandings and coping methods, real client self-development can occur. In neuroscience, the concept of neuroplasticity, which was empirically supported in the 1950s thanks to the invention of the electron microscope, helps us understand better what happens when clients are worked with from a humanistic perspective.

Neuroplasticity theory clearly suggests that as each individual grows, develops, and incorporates new learnings, his or her brain is constantly being modified and restructured. Consequently, the brain you had yesterday is not the same brain you have today. This scientific perspective fits very well with the humanistic ideology, which suggests that we are all *in the process of becoming*. New information means new neurological connections and both physical and chemical changes in the brain. Grey (2010) suggested that when a person is provided new information, brand new neural connections are created to entertain this new data. Garland and Howard (2009) suggested that not only are new neuro-pathways developed throughout the lifespan, but also, perhaps even more intriguing for counselors, that through experiences that challenge the client in a deep and meaningful way, the actual development of *new* brain tissue occurs. At its very core, the essence of humanistic counseling focuses on the opportunity clients have to learn new things about themselves from within. Obviously, when this goal is accomplished in counseling, there is the increased chance that not only will clients "feel better" but their brains can also be more fully developed, even expanded, as well. Additionally, beyond these neural connections, the brain also sends this new information to the sensorimotor part of the brain, creating new connections in that region as well. Over time, these initial connections can become actual reflexes (Grey, 2010). As a result, we find that the humanistic approach to counseling is supported by the current information arriving via neuroscience.

The Fourth Force—Multiculturalism

In recent years, the ever-developing field of counseling has continued to expand its professional journey in trying to better understand and address the true uniqueness of each individual client. This is especially true in regard to the issue of cultural variation. To this end, clients are more fully envisioned as having three primary layers to their cultural existence: *human universality, cultural variation, and individual uniqueness.* Of course, at least at some level, all counseling can be considered multicultural counseling. The very act of meeting to consider client issues and concerns brings together two people who have multiple ways in which they are different. And for its part, group work may certainly increase the variations almost geometrically. Nonetheless, even as we accept the fact that each of us is different from one another in a myriad of ways (individual uniqueness), we also recognize that simultaneously we are also all very similar in certain ways (e.g., we all breathe, we all eat and drink, etc.). Additionally, such similarities may be further demonstrated by the fact that the human brain typically organizes itself in a similar fashion from one person to another. The amygdala and the corpus callosum have similar functions for people across all cultures. What makes each individual unique, however, is the presence of energy, the magnitude of use, and certainly the style with which his or her individual brain has learned to receive, process, and derive meaning from the world. To some degree, such differences can be attributed to cultural variations (e.g., language, chemical changes in the brain based on nutrition, etc.). However, as we will be addressing in the pages that follow, the fact is that the uniqueness of individuals exceeds cultural difference, ethnic difference, or the like. Further, may we forward the idea that clients can be further and more deeply understood by adding the layer of neurocounseling to the process? If so, might we not then suggest that those clients who are significantly left hemisphere oriented are a specific cultural group? Based on what we know about the human brain, they would have very different rules and structure to their group than a group of individuals who are significantly right hemisphere oriented.

The Fifth Force—Neurocounseling

As we are certain you have guessed by now, we believe that the field of counseling is presently embarking on the first steps on a new journey of scientific and practical exploration using technologies unavailable to researchers of previous generations. Such efforts are being led by the combined and intertwined fields of both neuroscience and counseling. Although many authors have identified the fact that counseling can be verified and tested through pre- and post-test assessments and client reports, our field is now at a point in time where we are really beginning to be able to document changes in the brain as a result of counseling practices in *real time*. Through the use of fMRIs, client brains can be observed as different parts of the brain activate, fire, and/or become dormant. Further, through the use of both CAT scans and MRIs, changes brought on by clinical efforts in different regions of the brain can be observed over time (over the course of six counseling sessions, for example). These are very, very significant advancements, especially considering that until recently, we could only use self-report or observed changes in behavior to actually assess the impact of counseling. To be actually perched on the cusp of such potentially revolutionary aspects to neuroscience is quite exciting indeed.

Certainly, one of the most promising aspects to the advent of neurocounseling is the increased opportunity to really come to better know our clients. In essence, regardless of the style of

---

Stop and Reflect

If we, in fact, are on the cusp of a transition to include increasingly specific remedies anchored in neurobiological understandings, what will this mean for the field of counseling?

What will it mean for you as a practitioner?

How might such a transition affect counseling ethics, licensure, certification and accreditation?

counseling you use, your theoretical orientation, or your approach to being with clients in need, we can all benefit from better understanding the actual possible changes in the brains of our clients as we address and work with issues.

There Is Room for All of Us in Neurocounseling

One ever-present theme in the field of counseling has been the constant search for the "right" way to work with clients. Certainly, from its origins, Freud, Adler, and Jung debated and argued over which theory was best. Succeeding generations of clinicians were asked to choose between previous theories with the additional perspectives of client-centered, behavioral, and Gestalt therapies (as the main theoretical orientations offered to neophyte counselors). Practitioners who followed added even more clarity or confusion (depending on your view) by adding cognitive, cognitive-behavioral, narrative, and solution-focused approaches. Eventually, rather than choosing a pet theory or theorist, many practicing counselors decided to use a variety of methods (one from column A, one from column B, as it were, often varying such choices based on clients' needs). We call this eclecticism. Serendipitously, this approach may have turned out to be a good move, since as we start to understand the impact of counseling on the brain through a neuro-lens we see that each major theory, in fact, actually *does* present the possibility of having a positive impact on the brain of the client. Supporting evidence of changes in the brain has now been documented using data from neurological scans conducted during the counseling process. Such evidence can really only serve to better aid counselors in their efforts to help clients (Shedler, 2010). Simply put, it is another tool (albeit possibly a *major* tool) on your proverbial counseling tool belt. To date, researchers have been finding that a multitude of counseling approaches appear to have a positive impact on the brain chemistry and structure of clients, ranging from psychodynamic (Goldschmidt & Roelke, 2012) through

cognitive-behavioral therapy (Goldapple et al., 2004) to meditation (Depraz, Varela, & Vermersch, 2003). Of course, as we will
discuss later in the book, all of the main theories of counseling
can be supported through the use of brain imaging that provides
evidence of brain change in clients.

Given all the material above, we forward the following conclusions. First, the practice of counseling as an effective means of
helping clients "talk out" current mental health issues is an accepted therapeutic practice. And second, through the utilization
of modern devices and techniques which are expanding our understanding of how certain counseling practices may affect our
clients' brains, the field of counseling in general and, even more
significantly, individual practicing counselors will become even
better equipped to aid their clients.

Certainly, whether they recognize it or not, counselors, psychologists, therapists, social workers, and all other professions
housed under the umbrella of "helping professionals" work
with the brain on a daily basis. Whether addressing issues of
grief and loss, anxiety, depression, phobias, or the like, the
point of much of the work relies heavily on what our clients are
thinking and feeling and then how they might act as a result of
such thoughts and feelings. Results from effective counseling
typically cause changes, alterations, and new insights by the client, which then can result in more effective behavior. The brain
then—residing at the center of all these thoughts, feelings,
and resulting motivations—guides the behaviors of the human
being and essentially sets the course for the way the individual
lives his or her life.

More specifically, when we consider the brain and central nervous system, we are actually trying to understand the most complex piece of hardware ever produced by nature. In this regard,
neurobiologists aspire to more fully understand how the interaction among the billions of moving parts in the brain actually
form a rhythmic, systematic, and replicable pattern for things
like thoughts, feelings, and the like to occur. This is no small task

when we consider that not only are we dealing with the hard-wiring of the brain, but also the chemical changes, structural changes (which do in fact change throughout the lifespan), and the possible changes that occur each millisecond on the molecular level. This is truly fascinating and riveting stuff when we consider that without the functions and functionality of the brain as we know it, we could not read and understand these words. For that matter, we could not deduce, ruminate over, and reflect upon the connection between neuro-activity and the counseling process. The gift of being a species with higher-order thinking and brain development leads to the gift of asking the question, on a daily basis for some researchers and clinicians, how can we better access useful aspects of the brain to help individuals lead more productive, meaningful and happier lives?

Having said all of the above, however, let us be very clear on one major point: *This book is not intended to turn clinicians into neurobiologists.* In actuality, most counselors have never investigated, with any degree of deep reflection, research studies that delve into the inner workings of the brain. In most counselor-preparation programs, such information is at best limited, if even present. Further, in addition to the limited training counselors receive on the subject of neuropsychology, to this point in time, few of the major scholarly journals in counseling have published articles on the subject.

However, even without such deep understanding, arming yourself with information, facts, and understanding of what might be occurring within your client's brain as sessions unfold can make you an even more effective and productive counselor. The pages that follow contain a review of current literature on the brain and its functions and how particular counseling theories and approaches might actually have a significant impact on the function and functionality of the client's use of different parts of his or her brain. Such information then may provide a new and perhaps surprisingly important set of tools, which may result in more effective work with clients.

This book is anchored in the current literature on the brain and its functions. That said, we clearly acknowledge the fact that the findings herein should be seen as those of the *beginning* of a dynamic new force in the field of counseling. Consider, most educated professionals recognize the tremendous difference between what we knew about medicine 100 years ago and what we know now. In a similar fashion, with the advent and advantages of MRIs, fMRIs, and CATs and advancements in the ability to actually image and decipher the brain in real time, we certainly expect to discover significantly more about the parts, the chemistry, and the functions of the brain over the next 100 years. And that is one of our major goals in this book: to provide new tools for your use with clients based on the most up-to-date knowledge available.

Before moving further into the material, research, and knowledge acquired already in the field of neurocounseling, we want to take some time and provide a quick reference for the types of testing equipment available today to help us "see" inside the brain. These technologies, many of which have only come into widespread existence during the last 20 or 30 years, are the primary source of the real-time data that our field has long desired. Until the present, we have had to rely on self-report or behavioral observations. Certainly, these can be both reliable and valid measures of change. However, the new technologies give us the opportunity to explore aspects of the brain with incredible depth and clarity. Watching an individual's brain fire in one area while another area lies dormant can illuminate with great clarity what might be occurring inside the client's head as certain directions are taken in the counseling process. Neurocounseling as we know it exists only through the effective use of technologies such as those described in the table below. Linden (2006) noted that it has been a challenge really getting a strong handle on the working brain, especially in our efforts to detect true in-the-moment changes using noninvasive approaches. Thankfully, we now have such technologies in use and can understand in a much more meaningful way what is really happening throughout the counseling process on both structural and chemical levels.

Neurobiology has been around for many years and has made some startling and amazing new insights into brain function since inception. Most historians date neuroscience back to the ancient Egyptians and Greek philosophers. Many would agree there are two modern forefathers of neuroscience—Golgi and Ramon y Cajal. Each was awarded a Nobel Prize in 1906: Golgi for developing a stain that permits visualization of neurons through microscopy, and Ramon y Cajal as the first to suggest (using Golgi's stain) that neurons are individual entities and not interconnected (as purported by Golgi). As a field, neurobiology has come a long way since then; so too has the field of counseling. For some researchers, the time has now arrived for the two fields to be combined more fully to aid in the development of a clearer direction for clinical approaches (Creeden, 2009).

There are a number of items that we can identify as not merely speculative or conjectural but rather reliable and validated scientific fact. Neuroscience is anchored in considered, measured, and verified science that demonstrates the activity and chemistry of brains as they function throughout the lifespan. Therefore, recognition must be made that although we can consider our present knowledge of the brain as being toward the beginning

Table 1.1 **Brain Imaging Technologies**

MRI – Magnetic Resonance Imaging	Either 2D or 3D; displays the difference between differing types of soft tissue
fMRI – Functional Magnetic Resonance Imagery	Quantifies neural activity in real time by measuring changes in blood/oxygen levels
CAT – Computerized Axial Tomography	Provides "planes" or slices of the brain and its various structures; planes can be overlaid to produce a 3-D-type version of the brain
PET – Positron Emission Tomography	Produces a 3-D image of the brain

Stop and Reflect

Thinking back to all of your coursework at the undergraduate and especially graduate level in counseling, how much training, education, and reading did you do that specifically targeted increasing your knowledge and awareness of neurobiological aspects of the counseling process?

What parts of the brain can you identify/name?

How familiar are you with articulating how thoughts and feelings are developed and maintained in various parts of the brain?

Note: We sincerely hope you develop new meaning and understanding in each of these areas through our book.

of the process of discovery, we can also suggest that the conclusions that this book draws upon from the field of neurology are anchored in measurements that are far more than conjecture; they are empirical.

The counseling process is considered as much art as it is science. Knowing what to say *when* takes years of practice and experience (Gladding, 2001). Clinicians develop their own unique styles of working with clients across the spectrum of issues that they may face (Ivey & Ivey, 2003). It does seem clear, however, that most, if not nearly all, clients come to counseling because they are dealing with a life issue with which they are stuck (Cade & O'Hanlon, 1999). This stuckness can be described and assessed using a variety of different tools, instruments, and clinical decision points, as well as theories (Hood & Johnson, 2007; Drummond & Jones, 2010). Regardless of the approach taken, one way to understand the usefulness of understanding brain function is that knowing where, and perhaps within what region of the brain, the individuals and their life problems are stuck can point the clinician toward possible solutions and remedies for the client that are, many times, within the client.

This book will take you on a tour of the brain and its relationship to issues such as mental health, medications, drugs and alcohol, and techniques in assessing brain function. Along the way, we will cover the typical development of the brain from *in utero* through old age. Additionally, the connections between different counseling theories and their affect on brain function will be addressed. Finally, we have crafted several hypothetical counseling moments from sessions (annotated transcripts) that describe the impact of the dialog between counselor and client and how the client's brain might be triggered by different comments, leads, questions, and suggestions made by the clinician.

Neurocounseling—An Additive Feature—Not a Full Pendulum Swing

It is clear from current research that the brain is as highly advanced a tool as exists on the planet. In fact, according to Garland & Howard (2009), within the human brain there exist a mind-boggling number of connections at the cellular level (trillions of interconnected and intertwined nerves in the brain called neurons). The fields of neuroscience and neurocounseling are certainly in their infancy. Therefore, some very cautionary and clear comments must be made.

First, we believe that the brain and all of its varied components do not make up the entire person. There exist aspects to the individual client that exceed neuroscience and cannot be quantified or understood using current scientific approaches. In fact, some aspects may *never* be fully understood. For example, the human spirit, as Viktor Frankl so eloquently described it, does not exist in any particular part of the brain.

Finally, in the pages that follow, we have described and announced as best we can, to date, the present practices in counseling and the connections between neuroscience and neurocounseling. However, we are fully aware that as technologies improve and enhance our ability to measure brain changes, the field of

Stop and Reflect

The counseling process requires effective counselors to be self-reflective. Counselors are typically asked to become aware of their biases, prejudices, values, beliefs about human nature, and of course, their particular theory of how people change. But, with the increased attention to the scientific approach of asking counselors to consider clients from the perspective of brain function, there may be some who believe this may renounce or mitigate the understanding of clients from a holistic perspective. With that in mind, how might you fold the neuroscience of neurocounseling into your existing counseling approach that calls on immeasurable concepts such as the human spirit, resiliency, free will, psychic energy, and spirituality.

Second, although we will address the utility and brain-changing functions related to the process of mindfulness, the origins of such therapeutic techniques (e.g., spiritual and religious sects) suggest, and we agree, that the spiritual self cannot be quantified in any rational or research-based way that truly captures its essence.

neurocounseling, and of course the information in this book, is certainly subject to change.

So this book is an attempt to describe/suggest how counselors might better assist their clients in freeing their minds from psychological distress. Whether the issues are due to past trauma, neglect, life circumstances, ineffective learned responses, or simply the pain of significant damaging existential life events, freeing one from the chains of mental anguish and psychological torment is a truly noble cause. For counselors to better assist their clients in this significant venture, an increased understanding of the ways in which the brain functions is vital. We sincerely hope you agree.

Chapter Review Questions

1. How does neurocounseling *add* to our knowledge and conjecture regarding the previous four forces in counseling?
2. What does an fMRI offer that an MRI does not?
3. Make an argument for the inclusion of neurocounseling as a primary force in the field and life of the profession of counseling.

2

OVERVIEW OF THE BRAIN
AND CENTRAL NERVOUS SYSTEM

One of the gifts and skills associated with higher-order function in species (such as humans) is the ability to utilize words and phrases to describe incredibly complex concepts, processes, and parts of our world. In the case of this book, we will utilize this skill set through the introduction or reintroduction (depending on your current knowledge on the subject as the reader) of the basic language of neurobiology. This step is necessary in order to understand the parts, relationships across parts, and issues associated with the human brain in the counseling process. Just as laypersons may struggle to find meaning in a discussion between two clinicians discussing Axis II diagnoses, the language associated with various and varied parts of the brain, counselors may be unable to digest the chapters that follow without knowing some of the basics of the brain and its functions. Therefore, what follows is an introduction to basic parts of the brain and central nervous system. The remaining chapters of this book rely on the reader's ability to recall these parts and the associated language.

Understanding the Brain

Many people consider reading a very relaxing process. When I (Angie) read I like to curl up in a plush blanket and lie on my sofa. If you were to watch me read, you would see virtually no movement except for when I turn each page and maybe also when I make the occasional movement from my back to my side. The outward behaviors associated with the act of reading are unarguably very uneventful. What is amazing, however, is that the activity—or behavior—of the brain is always eventful, even when one is very still. Although on the surface it appears that reading is something that does not require much energy, if we were to measure the brain activity associated with reading, we would see a much different picture. As you read this book your brain is extraordinarily active. The vision centers are behaving in response to patterns of light and sending the information they extract from it to other parts of the brain for further processing. The sensory centers are behaving in accordance with the tactile stimulation they are acquiring from the book itself, and the motor centers are making it possible for you to not only turn the page, but also perform the eye movements involved in reading. Additionally, because reading is a process of meaning making, the process of making sense of letters, words, phrases, and such requires the brain to fire in various other, higher-order parts of the brain.

Stop and Reflect

It is clear that part of the counseling process is based on "learning" by the client. Learning can be understood, among other definitions, as developing new skills, increasing one's awareness of behaviors, attitudes, and thoughts, and/or better understanding self and others (including ways of being in the world). Consider yourself for a moment. How do you learn to behave, react, understand, and/or behave in different ways?

So if the act of reading is really a complex set of behaviors the brain performs, think about what is happening to the brain during a counseling session!

Before we begin discussion with regard to the various structures involved during counseling, we will begin by introducing you to the ways in which the organization of the brain is approached.

On the most basic level, one may discuss the brain in terms of its constituent cells, neurons, and glia and how information travels across the neuron to "speak" with its neighbors. In doing so one would probably also explain how there are many types of neurons, each consisting of specific parts that play an integral role in receiving, integrating, and sending information across the brain. For counselors, this view of the processes of the brain parallels what we understand as a systems approach to counseling. Just as in a systems approach to thinking—the entire system is considered from multiple views, levels, and interactional exchanges at a basic level—we can also consider the brain in such a manner (Racheotes, personal communication, 2013). Another approach to facilitate understanding of the brain would be to discuss it in a more macroscopic way, namely that the brain has two distinct hemispheres and that each may be further divided into four lobes. On the most general level one may simply describe how along with the spinal cord, the brain comprises the central nervous system. Whether one approaches the brain from a microscopic or macroscopic point of view depends upon the specific intent of the author. For this book, we feel it is important for you to have a general understanding of the brain at not only the level of the neuron, but also at the level of the central nervous system. This is because, as Linden (2006) suggested, understanding the depth of the brain as it relates to varied mental health conditions, allows the counselor to better fit clinically sound therapeutic approaches to the process. For those readers who are interested in a more detailed description of the brain, we recommend any undergraduate neurobiology or physiological psychology textbook.

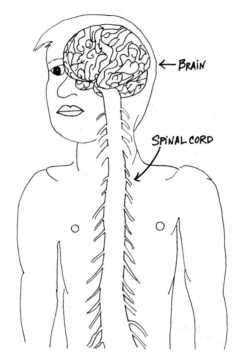

Figure 2.1 **The central nervous system**

The Nervous System—The Macroscopic Approach

The human nervous system is divided into two components: the central nervous system (CNS) and peripheral nervous system (PNS). The CNS consists of the brain and spinal cord (Figure 2.1), whereas the PNS consists of everything outside of the CNS (Kandel, 2000). This book will focus on how the CNS affects, and is affected by, the counseling process.

The Brain

If you were able to remove your brain, the first thing you would see is that it is divided into two parts, or hemispheres (Figure 2.2). The left hemisphere, also often referred to as the "left brain," tends to be more involved in skills such as writing, language, math, and logic (Iaccino, 1993). In later chapters, we will address

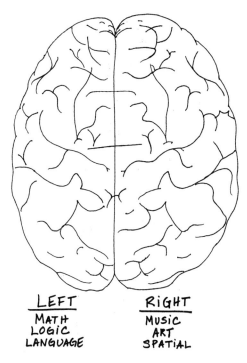

LEFT
MATH
LOGIC
LANGUAGE

RIGHT
MUSIC
ART
SPATIAL

Figure 2.2 **The brain has two distinct hemispheres. Although the entire brain is involved in most behaviors, the left hemisphere is predominantly analytical and the right hemisphere is predominantly creative.**

how, during a counseling session, counselors can encourage or in some cases discourage overreliance on this hemisphere.

In contrast to its linear-thinking counterpart, the thinking of the right hemisphere ("right brain") is more holistic and is involved in such things as creativity, imagination, and music (Iaccino, 1993). *Almost immediately, clinicians can begin to understand that knowing how and when to incorporate activities that involve this hemisphere can be of great use in the counseling process.*

For counselors, this information might seem intuitive. However, it is important to recognize that clients think in their own ways—and think about issues in their own ways. Consider the following case. How might a counselor use just the basic understanding of hemispheres to better work with the client's strengths in thinking?

Stop and Reflect

In considering your own ways of thinking, what hemisphere do you lean most often toward in your professional role?

How do you think you came to be this way?

What activities do you engage in that utilize your left and right hemispheres?

The client is a 32-year-old man who has arrived for career counseling. He has recently lost his job as an engineer due to a tough economy (the firm he worked for had to shut down) and wants some help in both the career search as well as in discussing "other" possible career directions. He is considering moving into a management position as opposed to continuing his career as an engineer. The skills required of an engineer (math, logic) suggest that this client is dominantly left brained.

Counselor 1: The first counselor he sees has had great success before with clients dealing with career issues, by using a life-mapping technique. She typically asks the clients to take time during the session to visually represent their life, and especially career, using colorful images, creative pictures, and as many different color variations as possible. The client struggles to "express" himself and his life journey in this way. Where was the mistake made?

Counselor 2: After not returning to the first counselor, the client makes an appointment with a second counselor for the same reasons stated above. He arrives, a bit more cautious this time, as the first session with the other counselor did not fit with his way of being in the world. He labeled it "silly" and "un-useful" to his friends. The second counselor takes some time to get to know the client and then gets out a piece of paper (at which the client starts to cringe). She then asks him to "engineer" a decision tree that he might be able to use to help guide them both through the process of job searching and career decision making. The client responds by starting to develop an engineer-looking blueprint of his previous jobs as well as future aspirations.

It is interesting to think that a similar counseling technique can have such a profound effect on a client when considered from the right and left hemispheres. This is the very nature of the brain. And of course it is a critical part of why we must, as counselors, recognize how our clients process, recall, and utilize information through *their* particular brains. But what we hope you begin to consider—or reconsider—is that your approach to working with clients, regardless of your intentions, can be either aided or significantly limited by the parts of the brain that are easily, readily, and routinely accessed by the client. In the case above, the major hemispheres of the brain *did* have a major impact on the outcome of the counseling services.

Stop and Reflect

In reflecting on your work as a counselor, have you had cases where you suddenly realized—or perhaps are now realizing— that the approach you took was a poor fit for the client? Knowing a little more about the brain now, how might you work differently with the particular case (or cases) that you can recall from your past based on your new knowledge of the hemispheres?

Cross-Hemispheric Communication

Just because a person may be "right brained" or "left brained" does not mean that he or she uses only the right hemisphere or only the left hemisphere, although there are cases of individuals who do actually have only one operating/functioning hemisphere due to disease or severe accidents (e.g., severe epilepsy, traumatic brain injuries, stroke). However, unless you are a neuropsychologist or work with neuropsychologists, most, if not all, of your clients will have two operating hemispheres and will use each hemisphere on a daily basis. The fact that one is "right brained" or "left brained" then simply means that one leans more toward one hemisphere than the other. You may be wondering, even though most people have two functional hemispheres, does one hemisphere know what the other is doing? The answer is a resounding *yes!* Despite the duality that exists between the right and left brain, each communicates with the other seamlessly via a collection of fibers called the *corpus callosum* (Figure 2.3). The fibers that comprise the corpus callosum are the axons of neurons. We will discuss what axons are later when we address the component parts of neurons. What is important to understand now is that a neuron's body may reside in one hemisphere but send a projection (its axon) to the other hemisphere to enable cross-hemisphere communication.

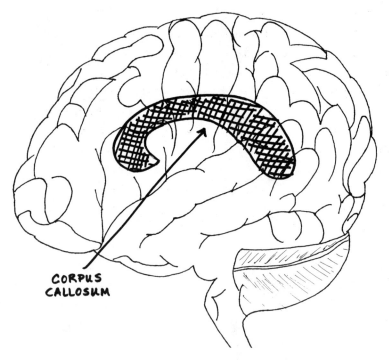

CORPUS
CALLOSUM

Figure 2.3 The two cerebral hemispheres are connected by a bundle of fibers called the corpus callosum (arrow).

One of the important factors to consider here is the health of and size of this link. It is estimated that at birth the human corpus callosum is comprised of approximately 200 million axons. This structure exhibits developmental changes until around 12 years of age (Luders, Thompson, & Toda, 2010). During this developmental period, the corpus callosum, like other brain structures, is exceptionally vulnerable to adverse experiences. Just as cars on a superhighway can come to a standstill due to a single traffic accident blocking the lanes, so too can the corpus callosum become "less effective" at relaying information across the hemispheres because of a single traumatic event. As such, a decrease in size or number of brain lanes, or axons, will most certainly affect the brain's ability to communicate with itself resulting in some level of behavioral impairment. Neuroscientists often use the saying "use it or lose it" to refer to how the brain keeps only those cells around that are serving some purpose. In other words, if a neuron is not used, it will die off. This is not necessarily a bad thing because in the normal person it helps the brain function effectively and efficiently.

This process can go awry, however, when cells that *should* be used are not. This is the case in child neglect. An emerging line of evidence strongly suggests that children who suffer from severe neglect have a significantly smaller corpus callosum, presumably due to some cells being pruned away from underuse (Teicher et al., 2004). Although the long-term effects on the specific children used in these studies are not yet known, anecdotal evidence suggests that the children will be more likely to exhibit a spectrum of behavioral and psychological problems than they would have without the neglect.

Early childhood experience may also contribute to the reduction in corpus callosum volume observed in children, children with Post-Traumatic Stress Disorder (PTSD) and Autism Spectrum Disorder (ASD), and nonhuman primates. (Jackowski et al., 2009; Villarreal et al., 2004; De Bellis et al., 1999) and Autism Spectrum Disorder (ASD) (Frazier et al., 2012; Frazier,

Barnea-Goraly, & Hardan, 2010; Piven et al., 1997). Rodent studies suggest that reduced corpus callosum mass is associated with reduced socialization (Fairless et al., 2008), a defining feature of ASD (American Psychiatric Association, 2000).

If the corpus callosum is the bridge between the two hemispheres, then the size of the bridge must obviously be related to how much information can cross at any given time. When a six-lane freeway must merge into a one-lane road, a bottleneck in traffic occurs. When this happens in the human brain, one's thoughts, feelings, and meaning can become jammed up, resulting in behavioral dysfunction, learning issues, recall difficulty, and communication problems.

Lobes

In addition to the observation that the brain consists of two hemispheres, another obvious physical feature of the brain is its bumpy appearance. These bumps are believed to have developed as humans evolved in order to increase the amount of brain contained within the skull (Armstrong, Zilles, & Schleicher, 1993). By folding within itself, the brain created a way in which it could grow in mass within a relatively constant skull size. The technical term for each bump is "gyrus," and the grooves between each gyrus are "sulci." The very deep grooves or "fissures" create natural landmarks to define specific regions of the brain. Using certain fissures, each hemisphere is divided into four lobes (Figure 2.4).

The occipital lobe is located at the back of the brain, is largely responsible for visual processes, and is shown to be highly active when one dreams. This is because what we "see"—whether real or imagined—is in part due to the visual cortex, which is housed in the occipital lobe. The temporal lobe is located on the side of the brain, near the ears. The temporal lobe has a wide variety of functions including audition, memory, and emotion. The frontal lobe is located at the front of the brain and is involved in higher cognitive functions such as reasoning and logic. Just behind the

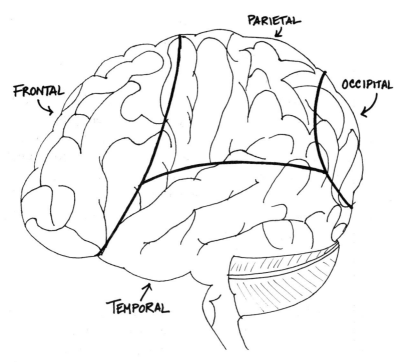

Figure 2.4 **The brain is grossly divided into four lobes. Fissures serve as natural landmarks to demarcate the location of each lobe.**

frontal lobe is the parietal lobe, which plays a role in our ability to sense and respond to stimuli. Beneath the two cerebral hemispheres is the cerebellum, or "tiny brain." The cerebellum is historically known as being critically required for motor coordination (Katz & Steinmetz, 2002), but recent research suggests it may also be involved in autism (Allen, 2005; Fatemi et al., 2012).

Note: Here we must understand that even though each lobe has several main purposes (e.g., temporal = speech), due to the inherent structure and makeup of the brain as an operating organ, each lobe functions *with* the other lobes in completing its primary tasks. Here we compare this process to understanding an individual holistically or as a gestalt, not just as unique parts that operate separate from one another. Counselors know that how a client feels both affects and is affected by her thoughts,

Table 2.1 **Lobes of the Brain**

Lobe	Prominent Activity (but not limited to)
Occipital	Visual processing Dreams
Temporal	Speech Speech recognition Memory Emotion
Frontal	Reasoning Logic
Parietal	Sensorimotor

so too does the exchange of material from the occipital lobe to the temporal lobe regarding seeing and then making meaning from objects in the world. Failure of the lobes to interact and exchange information would be like being able to see an object but having no response (emotional, physical, cognitive, etc.). Our brains are not wired to work in that way.

Stop and Reflect

As you did in regard to your lean in hemispheres (right or left), when you consider the primary theoretical approach you take to both understanding client issues and helping them cope with/overcome/resolve such issues, which lobe(s) do you most often target with your style?

How does your new understanding of different lobes and their impact on overall client brain function inform your counseling process?

As we delve deeper into the recesses of the human brain, it is imperative that we remind ourselves of two things: first, all of what we know about the brain is still fairly speculative. While advances in technology have enabled us to discover new truths about the brain, there is still a wealth of information that we probably do not know and may never know. *The second is that unless there has been a significant brain injury or severe illness, the various parts of the brain that we are discussing (hemispheres, lobes) do in fact communicate with one another.* In other words, these parts of the brain that we can separate for discussion in a book actually have an impact on one another and usually work in harmony with one another throughout the individual's life. For example, in order for a sighted human being to walk, at least from the brain's perspective, the individual must have synchronous harmony across the occipital lobe, cerebellum, and parietal lobe.

Just as hemispheric lean plays a part in the presentation and impact of counseling styles on clients, so too does the degree to which the client is immersed in one or more lobes. If you are like many other counselors, you have had some clients who came to counseling mired in emotion and seemingly unable to think logically or rationally about the issue at hand. These clients may also be stuck telling you story after story from the past in an attempt to help you understand why they are so emotional. In such cases, which lobe might be firing the most? From a neurocounseling perspective, it is probably the *temporal lobe*. On the other side of the coin, many counselors can readily identify with having worked with clients who can only look at the problem or issue from a logical, seemingly emotionally distant view. Does this sound familiar? These clients may be operating more often out of the frontal lobe. As with the relationship that hemispheres have to an individual's type of thinking and style of responding to the world, so too do each of the lobes powerfully affect the way stimuli, memories, feelings, reasoning, and the like are accessed during the counseling process.

Now let us take some time to better connect the lobes of the brain with specific counseling approaches/techniques. We will refer back to the previous table but now include some basic approaches used by different counselors from different counseling perspectives. Although we hope that many counselors utilize a multitude of different approaches and techniques, here is just a taste of what lies ahead in this book as we address not only the different structural and chemical elements to the brain, but also what may be employed by the counselor for a more systematically specific counseling approach.

If a counselor were to use an Adlerian perspective (individual psychology), one of the techniques the counselor would likely employ would be to ask the client for several early recollections (ERs). ERs are usually retrieved by the counselor by asking the clients to think back to before they were the age of eight and recall, in their mind's eye, an event that they experienced. Interestingly, for over a century, counselors have employed this projective technique as a means to better understanding the client. From a neurocounseling perspective, the lobe that the client will most likely access is the temporal.

Of course, from a psychoanalytic perspective, one of the key ways to understand and unlock the internal conflict within a client is to have the client recollect or recall dreams. In this regard, the counselor is asking the client to access their occipital lobe.

When considering techniques or approaches that most likely ask the clients to get their frontal lobe firing, we find both cognitive and cognitive-behavioral approaches to be very well suited. For example, asking the clients to think about what their payoff is for a certain behavior, directly accesses the frontal lobe.

For Gestalt therapists, having the clients come in contact with and experience directly their current state (in the here and now) requires a focus on not just what the clients are saying, but also what they are doing, what their senses are paying attention to, and how they are interpreting such stimuli. This approach calls for the clients to access their parietal lobe.

Roughly stated, each counseling approach, or technique, can be connected to the firing or dormancy of a particular lobe. Obviously, this is helpful since it respects and honors the client's neurobiological disposition(s) to "leaning" on one or more of the lobes. Further, in times of crisis, this understanding may become especially important because for some clients, access may

Table 2.2 **Lobes of the Brain and Counseling Approaches**

Lobe	Prominent Activity (but not limited to)	Examples of Counseling Approaches/ Techniques
Occipital	Visual processing Dreams	Dream analysis, imagery techniques
Temporal	Speech Speech recognition Memory Emotion	Early recollections, empathy, reflections of feeling, reminiscence exercises
Frontal	Reasoning Logic	Reflection of meaning, cognitive and CBT approaches
Parietal	Sensorimotor	Here and now activities, focusing exercises, meditation, relaxation exercises

be limited to one or more of the lobes as well. For example, some clients have great difficulty returning to everyday life after a significant loss. The overwhelming grief may become what Worden (2002) described as being *complicated.* In such cases, it may be that the overwhelming emotional response to the loss may prohibit access to the frontal lobe (where meaning making can occur). In Table 2.2, above, we have added just a few of the counseling approaches/techniques that may induce increased activity in each lobe. We will cover this in much greater detail in chapter 4.

Neuroanatomy

Up to this point we have discussed the brain in very general terms at a macroscopic level. Hemispheres and lobes provide an understanding of the primary divisions of the brain, which is a member of the CNS, but at its most basic level the brain is made of cells. There are many types of cells within the brain, but the primary cell is the neuron. It is estimated that the human brain is made of approximately 85 to 120 billion neurons, with

100 billion being the most frequently cited value among neuro-scientists (Herculano-Houzel, 2009). Neurons enable communication within the brain and also between the brain and body. Although there are many types of neurons, every neuron has dendrites, a cell body, and an axon. The dendrites receive information from potentially hundreds of neighboring cells and shuttle it to the cell body where it becomes integrated into a single message. The cell body then sends the message to other cells via the axon (Kandel, 2000) (Figure 2.5). A fatty sheath of myelin is wrapped around most axons and serves to speed communication. This is a very important element in neural communication and is well illustrated in the case of Multiple Sclerosis (MS), a disorder in which the body attacks the myelin sheath. Individuals with MS exhibit impaired motor abilities due to the brain's inability to effectively communicate with the body's muscles (Kandel, 2000).

The communication between neurons is referred to as an electrochemical event because information travels within a neuron in an electrical manner but is conveyed to other neurons via a chemical message. The chemicals that neurons use to communicate with one another are called neurotransmitters (Kolb & Whishaw, 2010).

Neurotransmitters are chemicals that are manufactured in the neuron, are released from the axon, and bind to specialized receptor sites on dendrites of neighboring cells. Neurotransmitters may be excitatory or inhibitory in nature. Excitatory neurotransmitters cause the cells to which they bind to become excited (more electrically charged). In contrast, inhibitory neurotransmitters cause the cells to which they bind to become inhibited (less electrically charged). In essence, the type of neurotransmitter released will cause its neighboring cells to either continue or discontinue neural communication depending upon the electrical charge it evokes (Kolb & Whishaw, 2010).

When we consider the process of counseling an individual who has taken on a pattern of behavior(s) that are unwanted

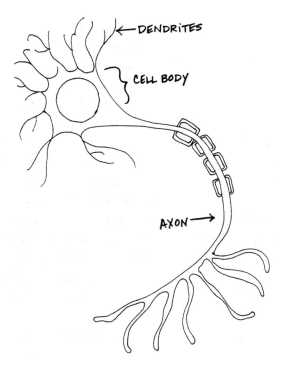

Figure 2.5 **The human neuron has dendrites, a cell body, and an axon. A fatty layer of myelin is wrapped around the axon to speed communication.**

or worrisome, we must recognize that, in fact, we are actually attempting to help the client develop new and more useful neuropathways. In doing this, we are trying to help the client rewire existing brain pathways at the neurotransmitter level. Current research is examining both the ways to best help such changes as well as the aptitude of brains to continually rewire based on chemical changes, environmental factors, and meanings made from life experiences. Such lines of research include study of neurogenesis and neuroplasticity.

Drugs that mimic endogenous neurotransmitters exist in natural and synthetic form. Alcohol is a great example of an exogenous drug that affects neural communication. It has been reported by numerous authors in the arena of drug and alcohol counseling that such devices are used by clients to alter their brain function and chemistry as a means to cope with psychological pain from past trauma and unresolved issues (Brooks & McHenry, 2009). Of course, at a neurobiological level, drugs and alcohol make sense as they *do* change the brain and therefore aid in the altering of the clients' views, thoughts, and beliefs about self, the world, and previous experiences. However, such devices are inherently ineffective in causing positive change to the brain. For example, alcohol is an inhibitory drug that affects brain structures required for respiration and other vegetative functions (Brooks & McHenry, 2009). As such, when one ingests excessive amounts of alcohol, neural communication in these brain regions may cease to occur and lead to death.

Recognize clearly, however, that this example does not mean that inhibitory signals are necessarily bad. In fact, both excitatory and inhibitory signals must be present in order for the brain to perform optimally. Seizures, for example, often occur because there is an excess in an excitatory signal in the brain. Without a balanced inhibitory signal, seizures would be a part of daily life. In fact, medication to control epilepsy is designed to inhibit the part of the brain that is overstimulated by excitatory signals. Additionally, in considering new tracks of research on working with seizure patients, a new line has emerged that includes fasting by the client. This is thought to "starve" the brain of the chemicals that are causing the excitatory signals that result in seizures.

Throughout the following chapters, the basic aspects to the brain will be discussed as they relate to and affect the process of counseling and the wellness of the client. Knowledge of the basics provides associated language to key concepts of the brain.

In closing this chapter, we want to offer you a guide to the material presented thus far. You may find the guide helpful and occasionally find it a useful reference as you read through the chapters that follow.

Table 2.3 **Guide to Neurocounseling Language**

Neurons	Basic cells in the brain that receive, transmit, and integrate information
Glia	Non-neuronal supportive cells within the CNS
Central Nervous System	Part of the nervous system that includes the brain and spinal cord
Peripheral Nervous System	All other parts of the nervous system other than the brain and spinal cord (e.g., nerves in the hand)
Left Hemisphere	Part of the brain focused on writing, language, math, and logic
Right Hemisphere	Part of the brain focused on creativity, imagination, and music
Corpus Callosum	A collection of axons that travel from one hemisphere to another to enable cross-hemisphere communication
Axons	The part of the neuron that initiates and transmits the neural signal toward other cells
Gyrus	Bumps on the brain created to allow for increased brain size within the skull
Sulci	Minor grooves between the gyrus
Fissures	Major grooves between the gyrus that denote/mark boundaries between hemispheres and lobes
Occipital Lobe	Part of the brain associated with visual perception and dreams
Temporal Lobe	Part of the brain associated with speech, memory, and emotion
Frontal Lobe	Part of the brain associated with reasoning and logic
Parietal Lobe	Part of the brain associated with information related to sensing stimuli and producing motor behavior
Cerebellum	Part of the brain associated with motor coordination
Myelin Sheath	Fatty layer of cells that cover the axons and help to speed up the dissemination of information
Dendrites	The part of the neuron that receives information from neighboring cells
Cell Body	The part of the neuron that integrates neural signals
Neurotransmitters	Chemicals made by the neuron to transmit information
Excitatory Neurotransmitters	Electrically charged to excite neighboring cells
Inhibitory Neurotransmitters	Electrically charged to inhibit information being shared by neighboring cells

Chapter Review Questions

1. A client arrives at your office with the general issue of feeling depressed. You assess the concerns, develop some rapport with the client, and start understanding the severity of the problem and possible resources for success and direction in counseling. You become aware that the client leans toward the left hemisphere and seems to operate more often than others in the temporal lobe. How does this last bit of info possibly inform your methods and techniques in addressing the client's concerns?

2. You are working with a client who seems stuck in the right hemisphere. Despite your best efforts as a clinician, she seems to only want to focus on the emotionality of the situation. When you ask her to process the problem from a "thinking" perspective, she looks at you in a bewildered way. You sense she is not being resistant but rather cannot truly access the thinking and logical parts of her brain in regard to this problem. What neurobiological factors may be present in this case that are hindering her efforts?

3. What role do neurons and thus neurotransmitters play in the process of sending/receiving information?

3

BRAIN DEVELOPMENT
AND BRAIN PLASTICITY

Brain Development

Perceiving physical stimuli, producing motor behavior, and socialization are a few examples of behaviors exhibited by both humans and nonhuman animals. While the similarities between animals and humans outnumber the differences, there are some behaviors that are exclusively human. Language, for example, is a behavior unique to the human species. Although many animals communicate with one another, no other species has developed a communicative process as sophisticated as humans have. *This is because the ability to perform certain behaviors, and not others, is based upon the brain we are born with.* Medicine has evolved such that organ transplants are a reality. While xenographic (cross-species) transplants are very rare today, if you were to encounter an individual whose faulty heart had been replaced with a healthy baboon heart, would you be able to tell? Would the individual's family report that his behavior became baboon-like following the operation? No. But what would happen if the person had received a baboon brain? Now would you be able to tell? Would his behavior change following the transplant? Absolutely. Whereas all hearts—human, baboon, or even manmade—are capable of performing the same task of circulating blood throughout the body, all brains are not created equal. In other words, the brain is what makes a human *human* and a baboon a *baboon*.

When I (Angie) teach my students about human brain development, I describe how the human brain is virtually identical to many other species during the very early stages of development. The fact that at certain developmental stages the human brain is indistinguishable from a salamander or a rhesus monkey, for example, is consistent with the theory of evolution—as is the fact that the adult human brain contains not only all of the parts of a salamander and rhesus monkey brain *but more*. That said, a person with a baboon brain would be capable of some human behaviors but certainly not all. He would no longer be human. Indeed, the human brain is the most evolved brain of all living species and is perhaps the most remarkable organ in the entire human body. On average, the adult brain contains 100 billion neurons, each of which makes between 1,000 and 10,000 connections with other brain cells. This chapter will discuss how the brain develops and changes throughout the life cycle from birth to age 99.

Birth through Adolescence

Nearly half of all brain development takes place by around age two with the most significant growth occurring during the first few months following conception. By four weeks postconception the human embryo exhibits obvious brain regions (forebrain, midbrain, and hindbrain; Figure 3.1), and by the fourth month the brain is distinctly human.

During the prenatal period of development, the human nervous system grows in an "inside-out" fashion. The emergence of a neural tube around 23 days postconception contains neural precursor cells that ultimately give rise to every neuron in the developed brain. These precursor cells undergo robust cell division and migrate out, forming layers upon layers of brain tissue. This process results in the oldest neurons residing in the inner regions of the brain and the most recently developed neurons comprising the outer covering.

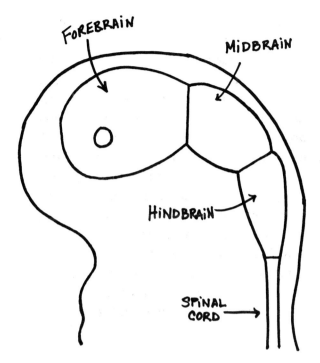

Figure 3.1 **Embryonic brain.**

While the newborn brain has the appearance of being fully developed, an infant's behavior at birth suggests it is still very immature. Given that brain development is positively correlated with the emergence of behavior, the way in which a child reacts with its environment is an excellent indicator of how well developed its brain is. For example, a newborn infant's motor coordination is very poor, but over the course of several months it begins to exhibit guided movement and eventually fine motor control. These changes in behavior emerge because the motor regions of the brain have developed sufficiently to produce them.

Jean Piaget was a developmental psychologist who believed that humans develop across four stages (sensorimotor, preoperational, concrete operational, and formal operational), each of which is characterized by the emergence of specific behaviors. In a similar fashion, neurobiologists operate under the assumption that changes in brain morphology underlie behavioral development. As such, it would follow that the maturation of the human brain coincides with the developmental state he/she is in. Indeed, there is physical evidence to suggest that there are unique and robust changes in the brain during each of the four stages.

During the sensorimotor stage (birth to age three), humans rely heavily upon their senses to understand their environment, which explains why babies tend to mouth virtually anything and everything they get their hands on! This process of assimilation enables the young child to experience her world. Experience, as you will read in greater detail later, is the key to brain plasticity. As such, the child who explores her environment through her senses is facilitating massive change in her brain. These changes ultimately lead to the emergence of behavioral milestones—rolling over, sitting up, crawling, and speaking—to name just a few.

Between the ages of three and six (preoperational stage), the connectivity between the brain's two hemispheres matures significantly, enabling the brain to communicate even more effectively with itself. This is evident in the child's behavior that has become more skillful and coordinated. During the concrete operational stage, which is between age six and adolescence, the brain is nearly comparable in size to the adult brain, with total cerebral brain volume peaking around early to mid-adolescence. Piaget characterized the final stage of development (formal operations; adolescence to adulthood) by problem solving and logic, which is parallel to what neuroscientists consider executive functioning (Emick & Welsh, 2005). Executive functions are higher-order behaviors including planning, impulse control, attention, and verbal reasoning.

The neurobiology of executive functioning is well established and implicates the prefrontal cortex (PFC) as its critical structure. Of all the brain regions, the PFC is the last to mature. Piaget himself acknowledged the importance of the PFC to executive functions, noting that the emergence of formal operations is related to the time at which the PFC becomes fully developed

(Stuss, 1992). One important executive function is impulse control, which is unarguably a very difficult thing for many adolescents and young adults. Bunge et al. (2002) performed a study in which brain scans were acquired from adolescents and adults while they engaged in a task that required constraint to be performed well. They found that adults had significantly more right ventrolateral PFC activity relative to the children. Prior to maturation the PFC undergoes a substantial pruning process whereby certain neurons and synapses are removed. While this may seem to be a bad thing, it is actually a very important part of brain development, as it leads to a more efficient nervous system and, in turn, an enhanced ability to regulate behavior. What counselors need to understand is that the brain is not fully developed until late adolescence to early adulthood and that working with clients of these ages may require the usage of expressive techniques in order to be successful.

As Landreth (2012) and others have noted, children and teens are not miniature adults. They are in fact children and teens who respond quite well to counseling approaches that utilize their natural skills and abilities in both problem solving and thinking. Counselors who work primarily with children readily realize the limited cognitive functions (especially executive) that prohibit advanced insight by the child. Rather, approaches such as play therapy and expressive arts (art, music, etc.) serve as the primary approaches. This is not only because these modalities are more comfortable for the child, but also because they have a basis in neurological underpinnings.

What Is Plasticity?

The invention of plastic in the late 1800s revolutionized the modern world. We are willing to bet that if you take a look at your environment right now, you will see at least a dozen items made with plastic. At my desk, where I (Angie) am working at the moment, there is a red cup, a bunch of Legos, a pair of scissors, a digital memory card, a hair clip, a tape dispenser, a few pens, a set of earbuds—you get the picture. Before there was plastic, artisans crafted each and every item they produced, a laborious and time-consuming process. My cup, for example, would have been made by cutting and shaping a sheet of tin into a desired silhouette. This was probably not too difficult for the skilled craftsman, but it did require some practice and a good amount of elbow grease. Today, almost anything we need may be made quickly and inexpensively with plastic. A single batch of molten plastic might be poured into a cast in the form of not only a cup, but also a Lego, pair of scissors, hair clip, tape dispenser, pen, and earbud. Because of plastic's incredibly malleable nature, virtually anything can be produced with it.

In today's vernacular the term "plasticity" describes something that is easily changed. During development, the human body is remarkably plastic. As we progress from infant to adult, there are myriad changes in every bit of our being. But once fully grown, are humans still capable of plasticity? Absolutely. For example, while our body height remains fairly constant, our body mass often does not, and when we become injured, our body makes attempts to repair itself. Although gaining or losing a few pounds and wound healing are certainly amazing ways in which the body exhibits plasticity, even more profound is what happens within our brain every single day of our life. Indeed, of all the organs, the brain is considered the most plastic by far.

History of Brain Plasticity

During the mid- to late 1800s, the brain was believed to be a weblike network of cells. Because neurons were thought to be fused to one another, communication was believed to simply flow continuously across neuron pathways to evoke behavior. This "Reticular Theory," described by the anatomist Joseph von Gerlach, was eventually debunked by Camillo Golgi just prior to the turn of the century. Golgi's novel method of staining nervous system tissue revealed that neurons did not physically touch one another; instead, each was its own distinct unit (see Lopez-Munoz, Boya, & Alamo, 2006). Golgi was the first to suggest that neural communication occurred via a tiny gap (synapse; see chapter 2) that separated each neuron from the others. Based upon his work, Golgi developed the Neuron Doctrine, which is still subscribed to today. The Neuron Doctrine states the following:

1   The neuron is the fundamental unit of the nervous system.
2   Neurons are individual units (not fused to one another).
3   Each neuron has a soma, an axon, and dendrites.
4   Signal transduction is directional.

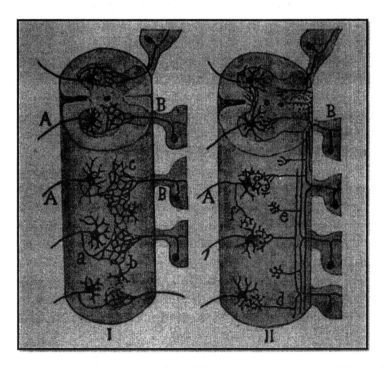

Figure 3.2 Ramon y Cajal's drawing of the nervous system according to the Reticular Theory (left) and Neuron Doctrine (right).

Figure 3.2 on page 47 shows Santiago Ramon y Cajal's (1917) illustration of the difference between the Reticular Theory and Neuron Doctrine. Whereas the neural connections in the spinal cord on the left are fused (Reticular Theory), they are separated by the synapse on the right (Neuron Doctrine). The beauty of the Neuron Doctrine is that it allows for, and at some level prescribes, the existence of plasticity. If our brain were made of a fixed network of cells as the Reticular Theory suggested, our behavior would also be fixed (and the philosophical question would become, at what stage or age would our brains lock in this fixed position?). The fact that not one single neuron is permanently connected to any other neuron gives the brain the ability to change infinitely. Whereas one neuron may "talk" to one neighbor today, it may decide not to talk with it or that neighbor tomorrow. It is this ability to make and break neural connections that provides the brain with an unlimited potential to change over the course of one's life. This, of course, connects directly to the art and science of counseling. The brain of our client really is not the same brain the next session. Period.

Stop and Reflect

When you consider the previous section on brain plasticity, how does that more fully inform your work with clients?

Are there clients you can imagine who might greatly benefit from the mere awareness that the brain is ever changing?

While it is impossible to actually see the morphological alterations that occur daily in our own brain, our behavior is evidence that they do indeed occur. The Mirror Tracing task, a common test used to assess motor behavior in neuropsychology, is an example of brain plasticity at work. In this task, a patient is seated at a table designed so that his/her hands and the tabletop are only visible when viewed in a mirror. The patient is then presented a double-lined star and asked to trace within the lines as quickly as possible. Because of the experimental arrangement, the patient must learn that in order to correctly draw within the lines, his/her behavior must adapt to the upside-down and backward view of the visual field. As expected, patients perform this task very poorly during the first several trials. However, with continued practice, the patients are able to complete the task not only accurately, but also quickly (Figure 3.3).

Neuroscientists believe that with every change in behavior there is an underlying change in the brain. That said, the initial trials of the Mirror Tracing task are likely performed by the network of neurons typically involved in writing since that network tends to work well in that capacity. However, when the brain realizes that this network is not sufficiently capable of performing the task to the desired standard, it begins to change. The network initiates a process whereby new neurons are recruited and others are terminated until the desired behavior is produced. Essentially, the network morphs into something completely new based upon the demand of the system just like molten plastic morphs into a cup based upon the die in which it is cast.

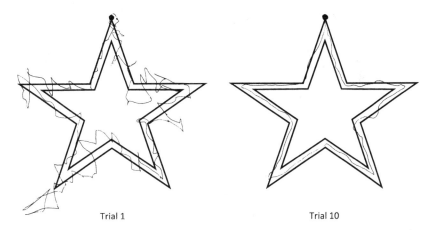

Trial 1   Trial 10

Figure 3.3 **Participants who perform the Mirror Tracing task initially perform very poorly (trial 1), but over time their performance becomes significantly better (trial 10).**

Consider another example. Let us say you were given an opportunity to join the circus and perform as a tightrope walker. How well would you walk the tightrope the first time? Unless you have had previous experience in tightrope walking, you probably would not do too well. Most likely, you would move very slowly and make numerous errors in your footing as you make your way to the platform. However, over many days of repeated trials, you would eventually learn to walk the tightrope with relative ease, making virtually no foot faults and completing the stunt in record time. Does brain plasticity really underlie your change in tightrope-walking behavior? Absolutely! In 1990 a group of neuroscientists from the University of Illinois designed an experiment to elucidate the neurobiological substrates that accompany motor learning. In the study, rats were trained on an acrobatic task (Figure 3.4) or walked on a motorized treadmill for 30 consecutive days after which their brains were removed for examination. The results revealed that compared to the treadmill rats, the acrobat rats had hundreds of thousands more synapses in a particular region of the cerebellum associated with forelimb movements. These results provide overwhelming support for the relationship between learning and brain plasticity (Black et al., 1990). Based upon this study, along with many others, it is now widely believed that changes in the brain must also accompany changes in behavior. In other words, each time you develop a new behavior—whether it be walking a tightrope or learning to knit—your malleable brain is restructuring itself to produce that behavior.

In our clients, we can see the same sets of patterns emerge and remain intact over weeks, months, or even years. For example, the use of solution-focused brief therapy (SFBT) focuses the client on positives, future hopes, and aspirations and meanings that are aligned with healthy and useful connotations. When a counselor uses this type of approach and listens intently to the client for opportunities to reframe the story/meaning, it becomes clear how negative and problem saturated the client's

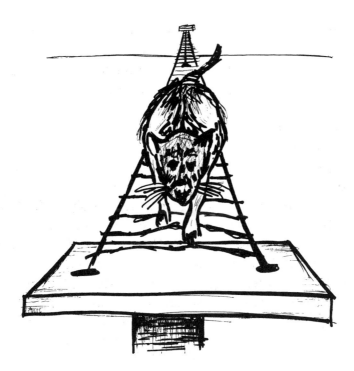

Figure 3.4 Illustration of a rat traversing a tightrope. The ability to move from one platform to another requires the animal to acquire a new motor skill and results in synaptic changes in the area of the brain associated with the rat forelimb.

story really is. Just as the rat develops *new* synaptic connections, our clients also develop, maintain, and therefore can create *new* synaptic connections across their life stories.

Brain plasticity is also evident following traumatic injury. The sensorimotor cortex (SMC) is the part of the brain that receives all sensory information. As I type these words, the physical stimuli produced by the keys are being transduced into neural signals that are sent to the SMC, where my brain produces the perception of touch. The SMC is organized such that every body part is represented within it. Moreover, this representation is topographically organized so that the pinky finger part of the SMC is next to the ring finger part of the SMC that is next to the middle finger part of the SMC and so on. Note that the face is not adjacent to the neck, but to the hand instead (Figure 3.5).

The topographical arrangement of the SMC was discovered by electrically simulating the brain and recording which parts of the body responded. These experiments resulted in a "sensorimotor map," which has been established in many species in addition to humans.

So what does this have to do with brain plasticity? To answer that question, think about what happens to someone who has had a hand amputated. Clearly it would be a traumatic experience associated with behavioral challenges, especially if the hand lost was one's dominant hand. However, think beyond the behavioral challenges and try to imagine what is happening in that person's brain. Do you remember how on the SMC the face is next to the hand? When a hand is no longer receiving tactile

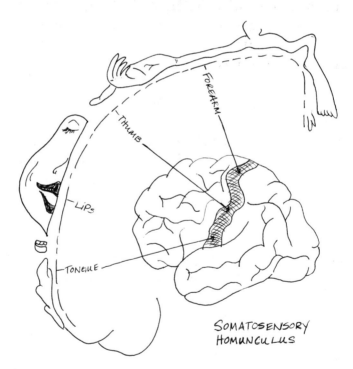

Figure 3.5 **Somatosensory homunculus.**

stimulation due to amputation or nerve damage, does that part of the SMC simply go dormant and unused? Absolutely not. The part of the brain no longer receiving information from the hand is reassigned to the body parts adjacent to it on the topographic map. Researchers have mapped the SMC of monkeys and then severed the neural connection between each monkey's hand and its SMC. Several months later the monkeys' SMC was remapped and compared to the one created prior to injury. The results revealed that the maps changed markedly. The portion of the SMC no longer used by the hand had been taken over by the adjacent face region (Pons et al., 1991; Kaas et al., 2008).

Perhaps one of the most well-known studies demonstrating brain plasticity is that by Wiesel and Hubel (1963) who examined the effect of visual deprivation on the cat visual cortex. The researchers sutured one eye shut at birth and three months later removed the sutures, allowing the cats to "see" out of both eyes. Several months later, examination of the brains revealed that the part of the visual cortex associated with the sutured eye was significantly underdeveloped relative to the visual cortex associated with the seeing eye. Since the visual cortex is organized in a columnar fashion, with each eye projecting to every other column, Wiesel and Hubel also used a radioactive dye to determine the activity of the visual cortex. The histology revealed a pattern of stripes overlaid upon the visual cortex such that the areas connected with the "good" were black (indicating activity) whereas the areas connected to the sutured eye were white (indicating inactivity).

It does not necessarily take long for the brain to exhibit plastic changes. When one engages in aerobic activity, for example, increased cerebral blood flow is observed almost immediately in traditional motor regions of the brain as well as in the hippocampus (Nishijima et al., 2012; Nishijima & Soya, 2006). According to Sikorski et al. (2012), the immediate metabolic demands of the hippocampus are likely related to more long-term morphological changes in its vascular system. Within only two days of exercise onset, voluntary wheel running increases the expression of angiogenesis markers in the hippocampus (Kerr & Swain, 2011), and 30 days following the initiation of physical activity, angiogenic markers remain high (Kerr & Swain, 2011) and are accompanied by increased vascular density (Sikorski & Swain, 2006).

Conclusion

Brain development and plasticity are remarkable processes. Within weeks of conception the human embryo begins to exhibit distinct brain regions, and at the time of birth all of its necessary hardware is fully established. Although the brain grows most rapidly during the first two years of our life, through our life experiences it continues to remain capable of change until the day we die. This "plasticity" is what makes change possible. Given what is known about brain plasticity, counselors can assume that real, physical changes in the brains of our clients are what underlie their behavioral changes. With that said, a counselor's work is truly "mind changing."

Chapter Review Questions

1. How does knowing that the prefrontal cortex is typically the last part of the brain to develop inform your work with children and teens?
2. How does the concept of brain plasticity inform your understanding of how clients can become stuck in negative or unproductive thinking/feeling?
3. Define and describe the basic concepts inherent in the topographical arrangement of the SMC.

4

THE DIFFERENTIAL IMPACT
OF DIFFERENT COUNSELING
APPROACHES ON THE BRAIN

Counseling theories provide both theoretical and evidenced-based strategies to effect positive change in the lives of clients (Murdock, 2012). Through different approaches, styles, and sets of techniques (McHenry & McHenry, 2006), counselors make efforts to help clients make meaning (Rogers, 1951), discover new ways of living (Ellis, 2001), re-author their life story (White & Epston, 1990), and enhance decision-making skills during troubling times. Though different theories have been suggested and even researched as being effective with certain types of clients (e.g., cognitive-behavioral therapy with PTSD), there has been scant attention paid to the possible neurological reasons for such connections between therapeutic approaches and specific client issues. In this regard, perhaps a better understanding and recognition of the ways that different types of counseling approaches affect the brain—and therefore the client's thoughts, feelings, and actions—can be quite useful for clinicians.

A note here that we wish to strenuously suggest is that although we often consider counseling and the counseling process to happen primarily between the client's ears, in point of fact, some counseling approaches recommend that the client act first. And through such physical acting, changes in behavior can lead to changes in thinking. Therefore, this chapter not only addresses attempts to change the brain through discussion, dialog, and re-directing thinking, but also through having clients act physically, and therefore change chemical, physical, and physiological aspects to both their body and their mind.

Neuroplasticity

We now have the technology and means by which to measure small, but sometimes significant, changes in the brain. As described in chapter 3, the field of neuroscience has, in fact, clearly documented that brains change throughout the lifetime. What is really important for counselors to understand is that the client's brain is not the same from session to session. This is newly understood knowledge about how the brain of a client changes both structurally and chemically based on life experiences, environmental factors, physical activity, diet, and other factors that affect living. Of course, counselors know intrinsically that clients' brains are capable of change, and that over time, significant new neuro-pathways can form regarding existing concerns, issues, and unwanted behaviors. However, this stream of knowledge regarding the plasticity of the brain showing that from moment to moment the client's brain is actually slightly different offers us new opportunities to utilize the neuroplastic features already in place.

In considering the connections across different theories with the possible effect on individuals' brains and what might be triggered within the brain, the number of possibilities appears endless. Therefore, this chapter has been written to address major concepts held within major counseling theories. We acknowledge that we are painting with a very broad brush. Additionally, because many counseling theories address similar concepts (either through similar or different language), we have striven to highlight aspects of theories that appear somewhat unique to that particular theory. However, before we discuss these concepts and how they affect the brain, it is important to recognize that when one enters counseling, he/she embarks upon a new relationship. The subsequent discussion will describe the dynamics of relationships in general and how they are markedly similar to the counseling relationship.

Interpersonal Relationships, the Counseling Relationship, and Core Concepts across Most Counseling Approaches

According to the Relational Stages Model, interpersonal relationships progress through a five-stage process that includes initiating, experimenting, intensifying, integrating, and bonding (Knapp & Vangelisti, 2000). This process and the activities associated with each stage, includes many of the factors identified by Lambert & Ogles (2004) as being most prevalent across many counseling theories that include positive relationship, reassurance, structure, catharsis, identification with counselor, release of tension, trust, insight, affective experience, taking risks, and reality testing. The following discussion will integrate the stages of interpersonal relationship formation with the factors associated with most counseling theories in an effort to emphasize their similarities. We believe that the high degree of relatedness between interpersonal relationships and the counseling relationship will enable us to identify the neurobiological substrates that underlie the counseling process.

After a client makes an appointment with a counselor (Stage 1: initiation), both individuals meet and discuss the client's values, beliefs, and expectations (Stage 2: experimentation) in order to determine whether the relationship is a *positive* one and a good fit. If the client chooses to work with the therapist, he/she will begin to *trust* the therapist enough to share the personal issues (Stage 3: intensification) for which counseling was sought, and over the course of many counseling sessions a client might *identify* with the therapist (Stage 4: integration).

The final stage of Knapp's model (Stage 5: bonding) does not translate directly to the counseling process, but still there are parallels. Whereas Knapp views bonding as a pair sharing their lives with one another, ultimately in some form of commitment, the bond between a counselor and client probably is best described as the thing that emerges from the process of intensification.

There is a substantial body of literature on the neurobiology of interpersonal relationships. Given the parallel between traditional relationships and the counseling relationship, the neurobiology of both is probably quite similar. It is well established that the neuropeptide oxytocin (OT) is critical to many interpersonal aspects of behavior. The majority of the literature on this topic has examined the involvement of OT in mother-infant attachment and indicates that it is required to form that relational bond. Rodent studies demonstrate that there is an increase in oxytocin receptor (OTR) binding in mothers that exhibit caregiving behavior toward their young (Francis et al., 2000) and that blocking OTRs reduces maternal behavior (Stern & Taylor, 1991).

OT-producing neurons are located in the hypothalamus (Rossoni et al., 2008) and project to many brain regions, including the ventral tegmental area (VTA) (Numan & Sheehan, 1997). The VTA is part of the brain's reward circuit and is rich in OTRs (Gimpl & Fahrenholz, 2001). The VTA contains dopamine (DA) neurons that project to the nucleus accumbens (NAc). When humans engage in certain behaviors—such as sex, taking drugs, and even eating chocolate—VTA neurons secrete DA within the NAc to produce a feeling of euphoria. Ultimately, the pleasure experienced from these behaviors leads one to continue these behaviors. In the formation of relational bonds, OTR activation in the VTA leads to an increase in DA in the NAc (Champagne et al., 2004), which serves to reinforce the relationship. Although this work has been conducted primarily in nonhuman animal models engaged in traditional relationships, it is likely that a similar process occurs in both the patient and counselor as they develop their relationship.

Aside from developing relational bonds, OT appears to also be involved in relationship *commitment,* another important part of the counseling process. A recent study by Scheele et al. (2012) found that men in committed relationships who were given a dose of OT tended to feel more uncomfortable around an attractive female than did men who received a placebo. In another study involving couples, OT levels were measured twice: once at the onset of the study and again six months later. The results revealed that OT levels had dropped significantly at the six-month follow-up in couples who had broken up (Schneiderman et al., 2012). Together these studies suggest a positive correlation between OT and commitment.

One characteristic of any good relationship, including the counseling relationship, is *trust.* According to King-Casas et al. (2005), the intention to trust is mediated by DA. Given that DA is modulated through OTR activity in the VTA, it is possible that OT is also involved the formation of trust.

Insight. Scientists are just beginning to understand the neurobiology associated with insight and creativity. Within this literature, insight, or the "Aha" moment (Kounios & Beeman, 2010), is measured physiologically using a variety of techniques. In one study, fMRI and EEG were used to record brain activity while participants worked on insightful and noninsightful problems. The fMRI data clearly showed increased activity in the right temporal lobe when people solved insightful, but not noninsightful, problems. Analysis of the EEG data corroborated the involvement of the right temporal lobe during the solving of insightful problems. However, the data also revealed that prior to the activity in the right temporal lobe, changes in the right occipital cortex also occurred (Jung-Beeman et al., 2004). What these data appear to indicate is that there is a specific sequence of brain activity (occipital lobe to temporal lobe) that precedes the moment of insight. The occipital cortex is our primary visual center. That said, these data suggest that visualization is an important element to insightful problem solving. Once one "sees" the solution, he/she moves it elsewhere to the brain to execute the solution.

Taking risks. Several brain regions are involved in taking risks. For example, the mesolimbic dopaminergic system, which is responsible for producing the high associated with certain drugs of abuse, is also involved when one engages in risky behavior (Reuter et al., 2005). The role of DA in risk-taking behavior is so profound that it is not unusual for individuals on DA therapy (i.e., to treat Parkinson's disease) to develop gambling addictions (Dodd et al., 2005). In addition to the brain regions involved in the dopaminergic reward system, other structures are also clearly involved when one takes risks. In one study, PET was used to examine brain activity while subjects performed a computerized gambling game in which they had to decide whether to take a short-term gain or long-term loss. The results revealed changes in the orbital frontal cortex and dorsolateral prefrontal cortex (DLPFC)—brain regions associated with impulsivity and self-control—as well as the ventrolateral PFC, anterior cingulate, insula, parietal cortex, and cerebellum (Ernst et al., 2002). In another study, fMRI technology found the DLPFC, anterior cingulate, and anterior insula to be preferentially active during risk taking (Rao et al., 2008). Together these data suggest that risk taking is certainly a whole-brain experience reinforced by the rewarding properties of DA.

Catharsis. Catharsis is when one feels relief from releasing emotions. Sometimes counselors assign homework to their clients, such as keeping a journal, to facilitate catharsis. Indeed, many people who journal do report feeling a sense of relief from expressing their emotions through writing. According to Liberman (2009), journaling is cathartic because it affects the parts of our brains involved with emotion and self-control. Specifically, writing about one's feelings tends to decrease amygdala activity (the emotion center) and increase prefrontal cortex activity (the self-control center). Another behavior that is also associated with catharsis is crying. Indeed, brain regions associated with crying include the amygdala as well as the anterior cingulate cortex (Newman, 2007). Although the neurobiology of catharsis is clearly lacking, the data that do exist point toward the amygdala as the primary brain region involved in the process. Perhaps this is why when clients have a truly cathartic event, they feel/recognize it at a primal level.

Most counselors will find the list above denotes many of the elements they strive for in both developing a working relationship with the clients as well as helping them more fully develop in ways that are productive and healthy (Murdock, 2012. Inherent in the counseling process, however, is the fact that for some clients, there can be great difficulty in reaching/meeting the above factors. For example, although some clients have the will to change a behavior, they balk at taking the risk. This resistance to taking risks may in fact be anchored in the *amygdala*. Thus, the counselor who recognizes a brain region involved in emotion, most notably fear, and that the apparent resistance is actually brain related and not a chosen behavior may be better able to help the client. In this instance, perhaps one way to help the client increase his/her risk-taking behavior might involve accessing the amygdala in a different way.

For example, if the risk-taking prescription is similar to that of the famous case of Albert Ellis (fear of talking to women), then the understanding of an overproductive amygdala can be reframed for the client in a way that allows them to increase their risk taking while not interfering with the important work of the amygdala. In this case, the reframe can allow the client's brain to understand the assigned prescription of talking to women as not necessarily being a fight/flight situation, but actually a cognitive-based (moving it to the frontal lobe, which houses higher executive function) research challenge. If one must rationalize this situation, it would require executive function and lessen the firing of the amygdala. In point of fact, that is exactly what Ellis did—and it worked for him.

Through taking the time to recognize that the client's reaction to the counselor and counseling process may not actually be resistance or reactance—but rather that the part of the brain that is trying to be activated is either unavailable to the frame of the issue or is overactivated—counselors stand a greater chance of utilizing the above factors.

Another way of understanding a clinical approach to this type of client scenario at the neurological level would be to lean toward classical behaviorism. If the client paired women (scary stimulus) with something he/she enjoyed, then perhaps over time the women would seem less scary. This is the essence of classical conditioning. If they are paired together, it is delay conditioning, which is mediated by the cerebellum and brain stem. This type of approach would also de-emphasize the power and presence of the client's overactive amygdala (Clark, Manns, & Squire, 2002).

Most counselors utilize additional techniques and therapeutic guidance offered by our primary theories (e.g., cognitive-behavioral, Adlerian, person-centered, narrative, etc.). Therefore, we have included in the following pages discussion of the major theoretical processes incorporated into different counseling theories. However, before we start this process, we must recognize two major things. First, there is considerable overlap across numerous theories. Second, and most importantly here, we are not addressing each and every different aspect to each theory. Perhaps that will come in later editions on this subject.

Stuckness/Perseveration

It is clear that neuroplasticity offers the opportunity for normal brain growth and development to assist in dealing with relatively minor issues clients face. Unfortunately, most counselors do not have caseloads filled with clients bringing minor issues. Rather, many clients arrive at counseling only after trying a number of other avenues (speaking with friends, clergy, family, etc.), medications (self or through their physician), and/or to modify their own thoughts and behaviors. And this is where counseling processes and techniques associated with accurate and clear connections with the client goals can have a dramatic and significant impact. It may be that although some of the client's schematic maps are seemingly rigid and resistant to change, they may in fact respond through the natural process of neuroplasticity alone. Through combining effective counseling techniques, those natural tendencies of the brain to restructure in positive ways may be enhanced and significantly sped up, resulting in significant positive client improvement. Neuroscientists refer to being stuck as "perseverating." For example, if you train an aged rat to learn where a hidden platform is in a pool of opaque water and then move the platform to another location, the rat will continue to swim to the old location even if it no longer provides him reprieve. The fact that the rat will not change its behavioral strategy is an example of perseveration, or stuckness. Cognitive flexibility is an executive function mediated primarily by the medial prefrontal cortex (mPFC) (de Bruin, Swinkles, & de Brabander, 1997), and alterations in noradrenergic input to the mPFC may contribute to cognitive rigidity (Tait et al., 2007). In 1993, Morgan, Romanski and LeDoux proposed the idea of emotional perseveration based upon their observation that rats with mPFC lesions continued to exhibit fear when aversive stimuli were no longer presented. This study, along with several others, directly ties neurobiological mechanisms to the stuckness observed in the clients we counsel.

Social Interest

One of the major components to Adlerian individual psychology is the basic concept of social interest. Adlerians recognize the power and importance of rebuilding, reinvigorating, and relighting the fire an individual has to be an active, engaged, and courageous member of society. Through such efforts, Adlerians suggest that clients benefit from getting outside of themselves and reconnecting with the larger world and people around them.

For many clinicians, such a direction makes inherent sense, as people who are troubled or discouraged can find new meaning in life through simple engaging with and helping others. And further supporting that idea, research indicates that meaningful social connections that are deep and profound to individuals can result in significant changes in both brain structure and brain chemistry (Rubin & Terman, 2012).

One explanation of how these changes work is offered by Rubin & Terman (2012), who reported the case of a client who has undergone high levels of stress over time. In such instances, the client may decrease neuro-connections between the prefrontal cortex and hippocampus while actually increasing the size and strength of the amygdala and orbitofrontal cortex (Figure 4.1). The latter parts of the brain regulate mood and emotional responses to

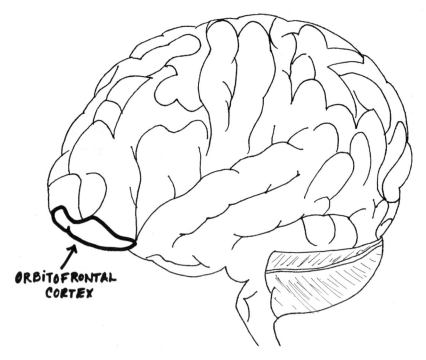

ORBITOFRONTAL
CORTEX

Figure 4.1 The orbitofrontal cortex is located in the front of the brain, just behind the eyes.

stimuli. Increasing their size could be a factor in clients who become increasingly sensitive to the world through emotional reactions. Rubin & Terman (2012) further speculates that, through increased social activity, those parts of the brain negatively affected by stress can redevelop the necessary connections needed for more normalized responses to actual and perceived stimuli.

Therefore, as counselors, it is important to realize that through increased positive social interactions, clients will probably develop more fully balanced brains.

Rapid Eye Movement Desensitization (REMD)

In this approach, trained clinicians utilize the natural processes in the brain to help clients overcome issues such as depression, anxiety, phobias, PTSD, and other emotional problems. The key to this approach is anchored in the body's natural tendency to self-regulate the day's events through deep sleep patterns that occur when the individual enters REM. Often the REM process is all that is needed for the person to return to homeostasis. Unfortunately, however, in some instances—such as fears, trauma, deep distress, and the like—the brain of the client is unable to totally complete the process and, over time, this continued failure to self-regulate these emotional and cognitive concerns can become problematic.

REMD works by mimicking the REM process under prescribed conditions. These conditions can include not only visually but also auditory imagery regarding the areas of concern and distress. In essence, REMD is an advanced and prolonged version of REM that targets problematic issues for the client. The core area of the brain this procedure attempts to alter is memory storage.

There are two general types of memory: declarative and nondeclarative. Declarative memory is the memory we are consciously aware of and can describe easily. Nondeclarative memory is regarded as our unconscious memory, such that although one may be able to state he/she knows something (like how to ride a bike), one cannot state *how* he/she knows how to do it. For example, saying that I know how to ride a bike because I pedal and balance does not really describe my memory of how to ride a bike. It is much more than just balancing and involves unconscious proprioceptive mechanisms beyond our explanation. The memories we are aware of may be of two different types: memories for factual information about the world (semantic memory) or memory for personal events (episodic memory). The memories discussed during the counseling process are episodic in nature. Clients discuss events they experienced and the feelings that accompanied them.

We all have a few vivid memories that we will never forget. These are the memories that tend to come up time and time again at family reunions and among longtime friends. Although we believe we remember the event in perfect detail, it is more likely than not that our recollection of the event is considerably flawed. To make sense of this one must understand a little about the neurobiology of declarative memory. When we experience an event, a memory for it is formed in the hippocampus, a subcortical structure located in the medial temporal lobes. This memory contains information about all of the sensory detail that accompanied that event. For example, your memory of your last birthday probably includes a visual of who you celebrated it with, an audible of the happenings during the party, and a recollection of the smell and taste of your cake. For this memory to become long term, a consolidation process must occur. This process is quite extensive but the take-home message is that eventually the constituent parts of the memory are eventually shuttled from the hippocampus to somewhere else in the cortex. Most likely, the visual memory is stored in the visual cortex (occipital lobe), the audible is stored in the auditory cortex (temporal lobe), and so on. Evidence from the rodent literature suggests that this consolidation process occurs within 30 days of the memory, as damage to the hippocampus within 30 days of learning a task disrupted the memory for it, while damage to the hippocampus after 30 days had no impact on memory recall (Rubin & Terman, 2012).

Person-Centered Counseling

The core concepts offered by Rogers (1951) in his theory suggest that there are several key factors that are both necessary and sufficient for client growth in the counseling process. Inherent within these conditions are empathy, unconditional positive regard, and congruence. Although counselors can operate strictly within a Rogerian or person-centered approach, many counselors utilize these core elements along with their existing theories of counseling (e.g., Gestalt, Adlerian, cognitive-behavioral therapy, etc.) (Murdock, 2012).

At its core, person-centered counseling typifies a *humanistic* approach to counseling. At the core of this theory is the idea that the client is in a constant state of trying to grow toward a more positive way of living. Although issues vary from client to client, a humanistic and especially person-centered approach work to help the client clarify his/her own thoughts, feelings, and direction regarding the incongruity between the life they are living and the life they wish to lead (Rogers, 1951). We now can measure the fact that person-centered counseling does in fact have a positive impact on the brain.

The very fact that we have learned so much about neurogenesis over the last few decades is exciting as it seems to further help us understand why some clients respond so well to certain types of counseling. Additionally, with the assertion that "regulation of adult neurogenesis is self-reinforcing" (Kempermann, 2011, p. 1022), we can now more clearly understand what Rogers and other humanists were describing when they said that clients themselves hold the answers to their issues. As clients develop a more consistent view of self, others, and the world, their problem(s) become more fully understood. In this way, the brain is better able to develop neuro-connections and pathways to both handle the current scenario as well as similar issues that arise in the future.

Solution-Focused Brief Therapy (SFBT)

The basic concepts inherent within the processes associated with SFBT include positive talk, reframing things (stories, memories, meanings, etc.) as growth oriented, and helping the clients imagine and then live life in ways considered more consistent with their goals. Primarily, with an emphasis on a philosophy that suggests to the client that they (the client) is in the process of solving their problem, the counselor uses techniques such as the miracle question and scaling questions to help clients imagine relief from their pain and problems. Research is now suggesting that in the field of brain studies and imagery, the simple act of suggesting that relief is on the way can have a substantial impact on how the brain receives and deals with physical pain (Wager et al., 2004). It is clear that such findings may be very applicable to psychological distress as well.

Wager et al. (2004) found that the use of placebos on the impact of actually perceived pain (e.g., hot handles of pots) was moderated by the brain based on expectations of the amount of pain the individual was going to receive. Using placebos for pain relief, the researchers found an intrinsic skill on behalf of the participants to ward off significant pain as their brain actually modulated its impact. Through fMRIs, it became clear to the research team that the participants were not simply acting like the placebo worked (as has been one of the arguments about placebo effects in studies), but that the brain was actually allowing only a certain amount of pain from the body's sensory features (e.g., nerves in the hand). While, in instances when participants expected great pain, the brain did not moderate the amount of pain allowed into the pain-sensitive regions of the brain, the brains of those participants who were led to expect little or no pain (not the body's sensory features) dramatically limited the pain and experienced far fewer pain signals being sent to their pain-sensitive regions.

This research seems to corroborate the overall perspective of SFBT in that pain (psychological) can be moderated and significantly altered simply through the use of effective and consistent positive discussion and new frames that offer hope and encouragement and highlight strengths within the client. Numerous researchers have found that through reframes and new insights into problematic thoughts/feelings, clients can experience increased organization of neurons as well as more rapidly form new neurons (Rossi, 2005; Centonze et al., 2005). In instances when the client readily grasps the new reframe, McGaugh (2000) found that changes in the hippocampus occur almost instantly (within hours).

Attachments and Stages of Life

Theories that address the attachment or lack thereof for clients to important "others" suggest that unresolved childhood issues can result in problematic behaviors. Beyond just feelings of distrust or feeling unsafe, clients viewed from this perspective are seen as having failed to develop the skills needed to maintain useful and healthy connections/attachments with others. Such limitations then are believed to cause many, especially adults, to feel alone and isolated and portend the possibility of leading to serious mental health concerns.

Numerous theorists have described and delineated different stages of life as people move through the lifespan (e.g., Freud's psychosexual stages, Erikson's psychosocial stages, Kohlberg's stages of moral development). Although these stages can often be spotted and worked with by counselors, only recently have we garnered the neuroscientific knowledge to understand one of the major issues involved in *any* linear development stage model. Although stages may be seen as separate, both Freud and Erikson suggested clearly that stages developed *upon* one another to some degree or another. For example, a client who fails to develop a positive sense of *trust of self and others* will probably struggle to develop a strong sense of *autonomy* (Erikson, 1980).

Neuroscience has now begun to more fully understand why these failed early life connections might really have a significant impact later in life. And, as such, these findings have yielded further evidence of the utility of counseling and therapeutic techniques with these types of clients.

Kempermann (2011) argued that one of the key factors in neurogenesis (the development of new neurons throughout the lifespan) is that "regulation of adult neurogenesis at multiple stages of development is additive and later stages are dependent upon previous ones" (p. 1021). What this means in terms of life-long brain development is that although neurogenesis continues throughout the lifespan, areas which have seen limited development will be far less likely to develop new neuro-connections. One way of understanding this process is through the metaphor of planting trees. If we had two different plots of land (say 25 acres each) and planted 100 apple trees on one and only 1 tree on the other, the likelihood over time of the well-planted area creating more "new" trees would be much higher. Interestingly, perhaps the techniques and theories associated with taking clients back to childhood and reworking their issues may actually be similar to the process of both cultivating the land as well as planting new trees.

Imagery, Mindfulness, and Meditation

Counselors sometimes use (in session) and/or teach their clients to use (at home) techniques that allow the clients to imagine solutions, new behaviors, and ways of being with self and the world that are different than they currently utilize (McHenry & McHenry, 2006). Positive imagery can be a very useful tool for counselors to help clients change unwanted behaviors. Interestingly, Pascual-Leone et al. (2005) found that neurogenesis in some parts of the brain (e.g., motor cortex) can be increased simply by having the client imagine piano playing. The practice of using the power of the mind to induce positive images and relaxation can have further positive impacts on the brain.

For example, mindfulness is present in many theoretical approaches, religions, and ways of being around the world (e.g., yoga, Buddhism, etc.). Mindfulness and attunement are defined as a meditative state when the clients are able to fully experience their feelings, thoughts, and reactions, in essence connecting mind and body fully in the moment.

The basic premise of mindfulness is the act of being present with both self and others. Seigel (2007) suggested aspects to the overall concept of *attunement,* which is akin to self-hypnosis, progressive relaxation, and being mindful.

In considering long-term meditative processes in individuals practicing *loving kindness meditation* (e.g., Buddhist monks), Lutz et al. (2004) found that there was a significantly increased amount of synchronized neurons. This state of neuro-consistency was suggested to be representative of both clear and integrated psychological clarity (Williams et al., 2005). Although this sample was of individuals who had been practicing meditation for years, Begley (2007) found that the neuro-synchronization existed not only during the meditative state, but also when they were not meditating, thus clearly suggestive of actual changes within the brains of the monks.

Cognitive-Behavioral Therapy (CBT)

The processes involved in CBT include helping clients to better understand their thought processes, meta-reflection on decision making, and linking thoughts and feelings as they result in wanted or unwanted consequences (Murdock, 2012). It would make sense that this clinical approach has an impact not only on the brain chemistry but also on the overall brain structure. In a study of women with chronic fatigue syndrome (who typically demonstrate cerebral atrophy), De Lange et al. (2008) found that CBT seemed to have a lasting effect. The researchers found significant increases in the gray matter volume in these participants. As would be expected, the increased gray matter resulted in an increased level of speed and dexterity in cognitive functioning. These findings support the thesis that CBT might have a positive impact on clients suffering from depression who might also have had (over time) atrophy of cognitive functioning (Goldapple et al., 2004).

Schwartz and Begley (2002) studied clients who were treated with a CBT approach that emphasized mindfulness. The clients, who suffered from obsessive-compulsive disorder (OCD), experienced substantial changes in their orbital frontal cortex as well as their striatum. These two parts of the brain are typically quite overactive in the brains of clients with OCD.

Play/Expressive Arts

The use of play has been advocated for by numerous authors as the best choice when working with children (Landreth, 2012; Henderson & Thompson, 2011). The overarching theory is that children will respond better to a therapeutic environment suited for their developmental styles and needs (Landreth, 2012). Current research, however, is advancing, going beyond the decidedly common knowledge of why play works with kids and searching to better understand what mechanisms are really being affected by play as opposed to a talk therapy environment.

Developmentally speaking, children's brains are *not even close* to being fully developed. In fact, some of the major structures associated with language (temporal lobe) and focusing (Grey, 2010) do not become fully developed until much later. This, in and of itself, may be reason enough to curtail trying to talk out issues with kids and allow them to play them through. However, there is much more to the brain of the child that allows them to both work better through play and have significant limitations in processing deep and meaningful language as we do as adults.

Blumenfeld (2002) suggested that the child's neocortex begins to develop at around six months of age and continues to develop into the mid-twenties. The neocortex is responsible for major facets of cognition such as understanding emotions, labeling objects, language formation, and strategic thought. In essence, in the process of developing the neocortex, neuro-pathways are developed over the child's life that connect the limbic system (senses) and the neocortex. As the brain and body learn from experience, these neuro-connections become stronger and more refined (Grey, 2010). However, since children are not nearly fully developed in regard to these refined neuro-connections, they are thought to be (from a neurological perspective) limited in their ability to process information linguistically or develop linear plans and strategies to deal with issues (Grey, 2010).

The primary brain functions that counselors can access fairly readily in children are through visual stimuli, emotional reactions (not necessarily in a way that they can articulate their feelings), and kinesthetic learning (Hammond, 2008). Of course, this makes great sense since the child is taking in information from the environment and developing the neuro-connections as described above. And, of course, such data allows us to better understand how the use of play therapy, music therapy, sand tray, and all other expressive arts therapeutic approaches are so well connected to the actual brain functioning and development of the child.

Conclusion

It is clear that the fields of neurobiology and counseling have a long way to go in regard to fully or even partially understanding the ways in which theoretical approaches influence the brain. Of course, since each brain is unique, we are not likely to ever really become certain exactly how each counseling approach benefits every individual client. This is true of all counseling, though; gray areas persist in our field. Nonetheless, at this point in time it appears that effective counseling theories that stand the test of time seem to really have the potential to have a positive impact on both the structure and the chemistry of the client's brain.

Chapter Review Questions

1. Considering the particular counseling techniques that you typically utilize, what evidence exists regarding the parts of the brain that such techniques reach/impact?
2. Describe at least two examples of approaches you can use to purposefully target specific parts of the brain.
3. What additional skills/techniques/theoretical underpinnings would you like to learn about regarding the impact on the brains of your clients?

5

NEUROBIOLOGICAL AND NEUROPSYCHOLOGICAL ASPECTS OF MENTAL HEALTH

Mental health issues range from mild discomfort to severe mental illness. Many of the more severe mental health issues that clients present with in counseling are typically found within the DSM-IV-TR (*Diagnostic and Statistical Manual of Mental Disorders,* 4th ed., text rev.) and, for the most part, are understood as being conditions of the brain. This chapter provides you with significant information across several major and prolific psychological issues. Although in some cases the genesis of the condition cannot be definitively correlated with a cause, by recognizing the part of the brain that might be located as the correlation to the condition, remedies and treatment courses might be better fitted to the client's needs.

The literature has numerous articles documenting parts of the brain that are affected or considered to be ineffective in relation to different mental health issues. For example, researchers have identified that the corpus callosum is significantly smaller in children with PTSD than their peers not affected with the disorder (De Bellis et al., 2002). However, a considerable word of caution here is that although there appears to be a correlation between the two, that does not imply causation, and perhaps more importantly, such information does not denote that *all* children with PTSD have a smaller than normal corpus callosum. We strongly suggest that you use the information contained in this chapter and, for that matter, every other chapter as possible guideposts and/or additions to your typical clinical approach rather than as absolute scientific facts that generalize to all of your clients in similar circumstances. As always, your professional judgment is still vital.

Top Down vs. Bottom Up

Before we address the individual uniqueness of different major mental health issues, we must start with a discussion of the difference between a top-down approach to brain change and a bottom-up approach. In essence, the difference is based on biological versus environmental measures of change. From a top-down approach, the counselor uses techniques and skills to help the client change his/her thoughts, feelings, and behaviors, which in turn cause change to the brain function and chemicals. The bottom-up approach uses medications to enhance and alter the brain chemistry and function, which in turn causes change to the client's thoughts, feelings, and behaviors (Kay, 2009). These different approaches are important to consider for several reasons. There is no one way to approach any particular mental health issue. Steps and strategies that may work for one person may prove ineffective for another. Often, as many clinicians have come to understand, the process of counseling is aided by the effective, carefully monitored use of psychopharmacological agents. Regardless of the approach (top down, bottom up, or the combination of the two), we must also recognize that in order for change to really occur within the brain, a certain systemic set of events needs to unfold. For example, a psychotropic agent might directly affect a part of the brain, or a counseling approach may, in a similar way, address a certain region of the brain (e.g., emotions in the temporal lobe). However, because of its systemic nature, in addition to these respective changes occurring in the brain, *other* areas of the brain may also be simultaneously affected either directly or indirectly. Taking aspirin for shoulder pain may have a positive impact on the reception of pain in the brain from the nerves in the shoulder, but the aspirin will also influence the thickness of blood throughout the entire body. In a similar fashion, chemical changes to one area of the brain typically result in chemical changes in other regions. Consequently, when we consider the counseling impact on various parts of the brain, although we may be attempting to target one specific region, lobe or hemisphere, other areas are also likely to be impacted as well. For example, increased focus on memories, as many counselors know, will typically result in the client having an increased emotional response (temporal lobe) and will also almost certainly alter the client's frontal lobe since the new information from the memories and emotions must also be handled from a logical and cognitive frame. A clear counseling parallel here occurs in the systems theory approach (e.g., if a father learns to handle his anger more responsibly, his changed behaviors will in turn cause all of the other members of the family to begin interacting differently).

Stop and Reflect

As a counselor, regardless of your place of work and role in the field, you must acknowledge and account for the use of psychotropic medications by your clients. The current research in the field of neurobiology suggests that meds and counseling may have very different effects on the chemical and structural aspects of the brain. Recognizing that "it all depends on the individual case in front of you," we ask you to consider, in general, do you promote the use of medications by clients, attempt to subtly prohibit their use, or focus as little attention on medications used by your clients as possible?

Neuroplasticity

In understanding the process of helping clients with mental health concerns, we want to reiterate how critical it is that we recognize the brain's remarkable ability to make structural and functional changes throughout its life (see chapter 3 for review). While it has been common knowledge for decades that neurons make and break connections with neighboring cells, it has only recently been discovered that neurogenesis—the birth of *new* neurons—occurs daily, no matter the age, in the hippocampus and olfactory bulb. While some reports suggest that neurogenesis may also occur in other regions of the brain, those data are regarded as controversial. Nevertheless, future findings may yield sufficient data to consider neurogenesis a universal phenomenon rather than a geographically isolated occurrence. The functional contribution of adult-onset neurogenesis is also controversial. While most research suggests it is advantageous (Kerr et al., 2010), others suggest it may actually be counterproductive since an already effectively performing circuit may be negatively affected by the additional growth.

While early brain theorists (i.e., von Gerlach and Golgi) held that by early adulthood the brain was unable to be physically altered, we now know that through different types of experience the brain actually rewires, grows, and develops not only new neuro-pathways but also new neurons (Lopez-Munoz, Boya, & Alamo, 2006).

For example, Maguire et al. (2000) documented evidence of hippocampal neurogenesis in individuals who drove taxis for a living. As a result of the need of these individuals to memorize extensive street configurations, the parts of their brains that help with spatial relationships, namely the hippocampus, become increasingly physically developed over time. Given that spatial ability and memory are largely hippocampally mediated processes, one theory is that neurogenesis in the hippocampus occurs in order to preserve, or potentially enhance, memory.

In a similar way, just as bodybuilders develop their muscles through lifting weights, this new line of research is finding a similar change in the human brain suggesting that through increased focus and attention on certain aspects of life, those parts of the brain most involved in such activity appear to develop new neurons and therefore increase neuro-pathways.

Another important differentiation being addressed through current research regarding the process and plasticity of neurogenesis is the manner in which these concepts relate to early life and adulthood, respectively. In the case of the former, the concept of embryonic neurogenesis is controlled primarily by genetic factors. In the case of the latter, during adulthood (including teenagers), neurogenesis is caused or guided by behavior and engagement with the environment (Kempermann, 2011). Therefore, for many of our clients, the process of developing new neuro-pathways, and of course neurons themselves, is regulated by both the actual events around them *and* their perception (personal interpretation) of such events. Here we note the parallels of these findings with the Gestalt therapy's concept of foreground and background. For counselors working from the Gestalt perspective, it is important to help the clients understand what items they are paying most attention to (foreground) and what *other* items they might also focus on (background).

To aid in conceptualizing this concept, Kempermann (2011) has provided a visual demonstration (see Figure 5.1) of a multitude of factors that can have a direct impact on the neurogenesis process in adults. The model below adapted from Kempermann's work describes and delineates a set of factors for just one particular client. Of course, each client's cloud would present differently.

A very important caution that should be noted here is that neurogenesis is not always a positive and growth-fostering process. In fact, clients presenting certain mental health issues—compulsivity, hyperactivity, mood disorders such as depression and anxiety, and phobias (as examples)—may actually use neurogenesis as a means to self-feed and further grow the issue.

Figure 5.1 There are many factors that are related to neurogenesis, and that may contribute to one's behavior.

As many counselors know, clients often arrive at the counselor's door only when the problem has become so severe that the client either cannot handle it or does not think he/she can handle it any longer on his/her own. Mental health concerns typically build up over time and therefore, as counselors know full and well, need to be worked with over time as well.

Are We There Yet?

Therefore, in terms of where we are with the information and descriptions of universal truths and universal approaches to working with clients from a neurocounseling perspective, we must pause and then realize that the field has no such guidelines. Consequently, as we continue the process of describing how understanding neurobiological information can positively affect clients, we must also continue this chapter with the notion that there are no clear-cut techniques or approaches defined through this process as being the "cure" or remedy for clients suffering from the conditions that follow. Thus, within each mental health issue section that follows, we provide several perspectives offered by the neuroscience field, not one definitive answer to the question of how to best work with the clients with such conditions. We will leave the absolute integration of this information in your hands as practitioners.

Depression

Depression is one of the most common and pervasive mental health issues addressed in the counseling process. From children to the elderly, depression seems to affect all stages of life. Additionally, although in some cases the onset or reason for the depressed state can be understood, in many cases there is no clear-cut start to the development of the depressed mood by the client. Many clients we see as counselors have suffered from depression for many years. Below is an example of a case of a depressed client.

Case of John

This is the third session between John and his counselor Fred. John has been previously diagnosed as having depression, and in their work together, he is exhibiting and telling Fred about many of the classic signs of depression. His mood, energy, and sense of lethargy are apparent as the two engage in the discussion that follows.

Fred: Tell me more about what it feels like to be depressed nearly every minute of the day.

John: I am exhausted. I think all the time about how tired I am and how I don't care about much in life anymore.

> Fred: Something keeps you working toward a better way in the world. I recall that you said that you felt you owed it to yourself and your family to get out from under the spell of depression.
>
> John: Yeah, but some days, like today, I just feel so down and I really don't care about trying and failing again. Nothing has really worked.

The basic premise behind the diagnosable condition of depression is that an individual has been in a depressed state for a significant period of time. The depressed state or dark cloud that the individual lives with day to day goes beyond what most people experience as being simply a bad day or tough week. Depression, through differentiated diagnosis, can be considered situational in some cases, while in others, long term. Clients experiencing depression may present with hopelessness, helplessness, depressed thoughts, suicidal ideation, physical pain, and sadness, and may move slowly and appear quite lethargic. While some evidence supports the idea that depression is a result of the impact of the environmental cues on the individual, other research suggests it may be caused by altered brain chemistry from within the client. As with many psychological disorders, of course, it is also clearly possible that the depression may include a combination of both environment and biology.

In John's case, if we assume further that, whether initially caused by biological forces or environmental factors, his depression has *resulted* in biological changes within the brain (which is the case for many clients who have long-term or major depressive disorders), it is likely that that change involves abnormal levels of serotonin.

Serotonin

For many clients suffering from depression, serotonin may be both the cause and the remedy for their existing condition. Serotonin is a neurotransmitter produced by cells that reside in the brainstem (Alenina, Bashammakh, & Bader, 2006). These cells interact with many areas of the brain, including the hippocampus, which is especially vulnerable to alterations in serotonin. In instances when the neural pathway that sends serotonin to the hippocampus is destroyed, the amount of serotonin in the hippocampus is reduced substantially (Moore & Halaris, 1975). The hippocampus is one of two brain regions capable of birthing new neurons throughout one's adult life (van Praag, Kempermann, & Gage, 1999b). This neurogenesis is significantly impaired when serotonin in the hippocampus is reduced (Brezun & Daszuta, 2000). Although the exact reason for this neurogenesis in this hippocampus is unknown, it may be that it functions to regulate mood (Kempermann et al., 2003). Support for this hypothesis regarding mood comes from brain imaging studies, which consistently reveal that depressed individuals have a substantially reduced hippocampal volume (Sahay & Hen, 2007).

If hippocampal neurogenesis is a biological basis for a major depressive disorder, treatment may seem to be as simple as prescribing exercise, which has been shown to significantly increase

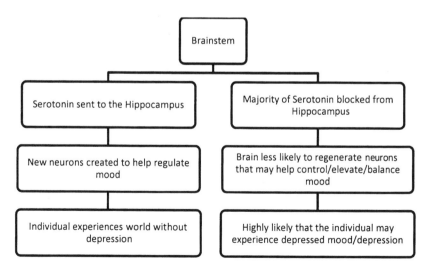

Figure 5.2 **Possible serotonin paths in the brain**

the rate of neural proliferation in the hippocampus (van Praag et al., 1999a). Of course, as clinicians, we recognize that such a prescription is not as simple as it sounds. Ironically, someone who is suffering from a true depressed mood typically does not have the energy to get up and exercise. However, through the use of both sound clinical approaches (e.g., CBT) and perhaps effective pharmaceutical agents, the actual brain chemistry can be re-altered to a more effective and efficient state of balance of serotonin. Evidence suggests that if John engages in physical activity, along with the use of effective medications and/or the process of useful counseling, his hippocampus will increase its rate of birthing new neurons. If John is also prescribed an antidepressant, the rate of neurogenesis is likely to be even greater. Not surprisingly, those who exercise exhibit an improvement in mood, much like those who take antidepressant medication. Both treatments have the same effect at the neurobiological level—both increase neurogenesis. Additionally, with the additional positive neural activity and increased chemical balance in his brain, John is probably going to be more responsive to and better able to respond to effective counseling interventions.

In addition to the "serotonin hypothesis" of depression, evidence also suggests that stress plays a major role in the onset of the disorder. Stress has been shown to not only lead to the atrophy of hippocampal cells (McEwen, 2000), but also mediate the stress response (Sahay & Hen, 2007). Therefore, there might exist, at least for some clients, a cycle of brain function that continually feeds itself into an increasingly strong and resistant state of depression.

Depression—smaller hippocampus—poor control over stress—increase in stress—neural toxicity is a cyclic relationship being experienced by many clients who suffer from depressed mood and major depressive disorders. One of the considerations here for counselors (and really any professional who works with clients experiencing depression) is that if, in fact, the cycle above is true, then when clients report that they cannot get out of bed

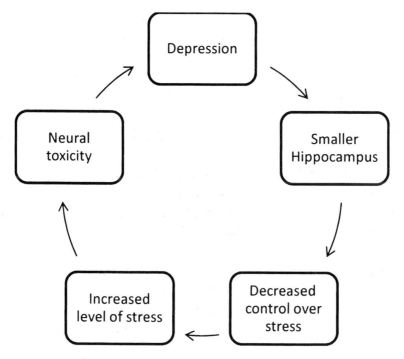

Figure 5.3 Cycle of brain function in clients with depression

or that they just cannot go on, they may be expressing truly elevated levels of neural toxicity, toxicity that from a biological perspective has increased to a level beyond their control. Though this does not sound hopeful, it does shed light on why people may attempt or commit suicide to end the pain. From a neurobiological perspective, this cycle can be devastatingly painful as the toxins build up in the client's brain.

Anxiety

To be sure, the human experience relies, at some level and some degree, on the effective use of anxiety. Anxiety helps us get a move on projects, activities, and daily living. That being said, some clients will present behaviors, thought patterns, and associated activities that go well beyond the usefulness of healthy anxiety (ineffective anxiety). Barlow (2002) recognizes the ineffective anxiety of some clients as containing a fixation on the current and, even more importantly, the future with focused presupposition of negative effects and consequences. In diagnostic terms, we can include the concept of rumination and significant impairment of current life events (American Psychiatric Association, 2000). Other additional facets of negative anxiety include thoughts of future threats (often unanchored in reality) as well as both muscular and physiological responses.

The following is a brief dialogue with a client suffering from an increased arousal state of anxiety.

Case of Jennifer

Jennifer is an aspiring graduate student. She works very hard at her studies and has been rewarded for her efforts with all A's in her undergraduate and graduate classes. She spends lots of time studying and reading up for classes. Having just entered graduate school, she finds that the demands on her time have started to take their toll. She is no longer able to balance school and her ever-intensifying personal life. She struggled with anxiety in high school when she was the captain of the cheer squad, on the debate team, and first seat flute. During the first session with her new counselor Amy, Jennifer both discusses and demonstrates her anxiety.

Amy: Hi Jennifer. I am glad we are able to get started today. I know we spoke on the phone about what has been going on with you lately, but I wonder what brings you here today?

Jennifer: (*in a fast-paced, rushed, and high-pitched voice exclaims*) First off, I am so sorry that I am a few minutes late. I mean, that is really not like me. I appreciate your time and do not want you to think that I am taking this for granted or anything like that. (*As she finishes the last statement, she is nearly out of breath.*)

Depression and anxiety are considered by many clinicians to be sister disorders. It has been hypothesized that these two disorders exist on the same continuum. Heightened anxiety can often manifest in behaviors such as lethargy, decreased energy, and a sense of despair, which mimic depression characteristics. As with depression, anxious behavior may be due to one's environment (a learned response), one's biology, or a combination of the two. Also, as with depression, anxiety is a disorder characterized by reduced levels of serotonin in the brain, and therefore, drugs used to treat anxiety increase serotonin in the brain. What seems to differentiate anxiety from depression, however, is that while depression is due to a lack of serotonin in the hippocampus, anxiety is produced by a lack of serotonin in the amygdala, the brain structure typically associated with fear.

The amygdala is considered an *older* region of the brain. In fact, this area seems to hold genetic coding and control activities directly related to our ancestors—from many millions of years ago. As a part of the "reptilian brain," the amygdala activation increases anxiety. This makes some sense when you consider the need for reptiles to always be on guard and attuned to their surroundings with a watchful eye toward anything that might cause them harm. In today's world, however, overstimulation of this part of the brain is considered the primary cause of heightened or clinical anxiety in people.

For Jennifer, regardless of the onset of the anxiety, it may be that her amygdala is working overtime at this point. Several approaches might be quite effective with Jennifer, including counseling, increased physical activity, and perhaps the careful and judicious use of medications. One of the recognized remedies used to cope with stress is exercise. Although it might appear counterproductive to prescribe exercise to someone who has a hyperactive "always running mind," in actuality, many clients report that through such efforts, they "run the stress away." In reality, what they are really doing is increasing the production of serotonin as they trigger other parts of the brain to overcome the increased activity of the amygdala.

Kjernisted (2006) suggested that as many as 85% of clients who presented with depression also exhibited strong signs of a diagnosed level of anxiety. This seemingly paradoxical relationship between these two mood disorders is further demonstrated by the clustered symptoms that tend to mimic one another. Further, although there is clearly a marked difference between the behavioral and cognitive outcomes of these disorders, it is striking to consider that both disorders respond similarly to certain types of psychotropic remedies.

Kjernisted (2006) reported that antidepressants with serotonergic and noradrenergic effects affect the inner workings of the brain in a similar way. That effect being highlighted by the fact that this classification of medications actually, especially in regard to the norepinephrine, serve to enhance neuro-circuit transmission by limiting the extreme "noise" of neurotransmitters that cause escalated effects of either anxiety or depression.

In a recent research study, Parihar et al. (2011) found a possible link between hippocampal neurogenesis and what they described as predictable chronic mild stress (PCMS). Armed with the operating hypothesis that the hippocampus has a direct impact on regulating mood, these researchers assessed the neurogenetic outcomes between predictable mild stress and unpredictable chronic stress (UCS) in rats. In essence, the degree of stress experienced along with the fashion in which the onset of stress occurred (e.g., predictable = work-related stress vs. unpredictable = experiencing domestic abuse) resulted in either hippocampal neurogenesis or atrophy. The former, hippocampal neurogenesis, also was found to result in increased cognitive skills and memory. Conversely, hippocampal atrophy resulted in the significantly diminished survival of newly formed neurons in the hippocampus. Thus, the brains of clients who experience unpredictable, chronic stress may have less neuroplasticity. One significant caveat here for counselors—it is important to note that *mild stress experienced by the client under routine environmental conditions may have a strong positive impact* on their *development of new neurons and neuro-pathways.*

Autism Spectrum Disorder (ASD)

Clinicians who work with individuals diagnosed with autism or Asperger's disorder recognize immediately that these children/adults have great difficulty with both common forms of communication and relational/social skills typically observed in individuals. There is compelling evidence to suggest dysfunctional communication within the brain contributes to Autism Spectrum Disorder. The neurons of the brain talk to one another by sending neural messages. Although there are some exceptions, neural messages generally travel along the axon away from the cell body and toward its terminal button where the signal diffuses across the extracellular space. This signal is then received by neighboring cells that relay the message to other cells. The speed with which neural signals travel is largely assisted by the thin layer of fatty tissue that surrounds the neuron's axon. As a comparison, think about what would happen if you tried to slide across a carpeted floor to deliver a letter to a person at the other end of the room. You probably would not get very far, and if you were able to slide at all, you would have to slide several more times to reach your friend. Now consider what would happen if we saturated that same floor with a layer of butter. You would probably slide very easily, quickly, needing only one slide to get you to your friend. The same logic applies to neural communication. The fatty layer that surrounds the axon provides a slick surface enabling the signal to more efficiently travel from one end of the cell to the other. Why is this important, and what does it have to do with autism?

It is extremely important because imaging studies show that autistic brains have reduced white matter. Specific parts of the autistic brain exhibiting reduced white matter include the cerebellum (McAlonan et al., 2005 and corpus callosum (Casanova et al., 2009). The connectivity theory (Just et al., 2004) suggests that autism then is a condition resulting from dysfunctional communication throughout the brain. Given that the primary way in which the right and left brains talk to one another is through the corpus callosum, it is logical to assume that the corpus callosum is different in individuals with Autism Spectrum Disorder. And, supporting such logic, research does suggest that the volume of the autistic corpus callosum is substantially reduced (Casanova et al., 2009; Alexander et al., 2007).

Figure 5.4 below indicates a rough representation of what some individuals diagnosed as having autism or Asperger's disorder experience within their brain structures. The failure or diminished ability of the corpus callosum to regulate and communicate across hemispheres leaves clients with the imbalance of information, often times leading to frustration. While the right hemisphere may contain more information and "skill" in understanding and functioning in life, the left hemisphere does not balance out because of the limited connection between the two.

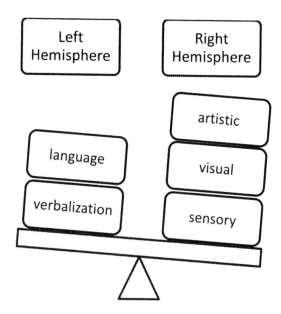

Figure 5.4 **Imbalanced hemispheric brain function**

The figure also suggests effective and useful mechanisms to both communicate with clients with Autism Spectrum Disorder and help them lead effective lives. In many cases, creating and maintaining effective charts, visual cues, and clear imagery to help clients communicate and understand communications can be quite effective (J. Lance, personal communication, 2012).

Post-traumatic Stress Disorder (PTSD)

Cook-Cottone (2004) found that nearly a quarter of all children have experienced a traumatic event by the time they reach adulthood, and of this substantial number, it is estimated that 30% meet the diagnostic criteria for clinical PTSD. It is further

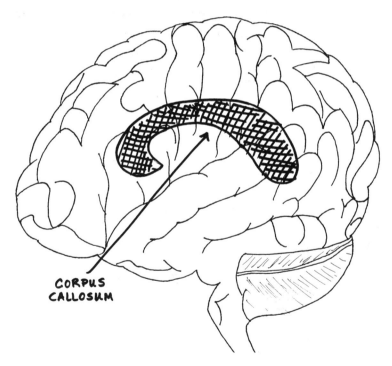

CORPUS
CALLOSUM

Figure 5.5 The corpus callosum is a bundle of nerve fibers located deep within the center of the brain that connects the right and left hemisphere. Research suggests that the size of the corpus callosum is reduced in children with PTSD.

hypothesized that if left undiagnosed or untreated in childhood, PTSD is likely to persist into adulthood.

Studies using MRI have found abnormal brain developmental patterns in clients suffering from PTSD (Jackowski et al., 2009). Important to note here, however, is that the abnormalities found in children differ from those of adults. Adult PTSD abnormalities were found to reside most consistently in the area of the hippocampus—a part of the brain that is involved in memory. Images of children, on the other hand, indicated abnormalities in the corpus callosum—a part of the brain involved in processing emotional stimuli and various aspects of memory (Figure 5.5).

Whether the client is a child suffering from PTSD as a result of childhood abuse and neglect or a war veteran returning home, PTSD has a dramatic and substantial effect on the individual's everyday life. The following mini transcript is from a case of a returning military member.

Case of Jed

Returning from the war was hard for Jed. He had enlisted initially out of a sense of duty and then found a substantial sense of duty with the other folks in his platoon. Having been back for about six months, he was still having trouble shaking the "cobwebs" from his service. He had been in several key and particularly gruesome battles. Though he survived, having lost only one leg, many of his brothers and sisters were either more severely damaged or killed in action. He used this as his mantra regarding his service: "I was one of the lucky ones." He would say it to anyone who suggested it must have been tough to come home. His counselor, a recent graduate from the local university, was still learning. She was a good student with good clinical skills. But during this session, she would miss a great opportunity to discuss Jed's real experience in the war.

> Jed: I know that I am supposed to be getting something from this . . . but I don't really think I need counseling.
>
> Lucy: OK, so I hear you saying that you are not convinced that you need to be counseled.
>
> Jed: Right.
>
> Lucy, being a bit unsure of where to go next, leaned forward and while fumbling around with some papers, she knocked her glass of water onto the hard floor. The glass hit the floor, smashed to pieces, and made a loud "bang" in the process. Flustered and embarrassed, Lucy missed Jed's reaction to the booming sound in his head.

Although a glass dropping to the floor may appear to most as a relatively benign incident, an individual with PTSD may perceive it as something much more threatening. Individuals affected by PTSD typically exhibit profound reactions to otherwise neutral stimuli and as a result may become so incapacitated they can no longer leave their homes. Given that at the heart of PTSD is a memory based in profound fear, it is not surprising that the same brain regions involved in anxiety are also involved in PTSD. The amygdala, which is critically involved in fear memory, plays an obvious role in PTSD (Bremner, 2006), as does the hippocampus (Shin, Rauch, & Pitman, 2006). Brain imaging suggests that the hippocampi of individuals with PTSD are generally smaller in volume than healthy individuals and subsequently function at a lower level (Bremner, 2006). In contrast to the negative hippocampal symptoms, in the amygdala there is an increase in cerebral blood flow (Bremner, 2006; Shin et al., 2004). This positive symptom supports the notion that PTSD, like anxiety, has to do with overactivity of the amygdala.

In addition to structural and functional changes in the brains of PTSD patients, chemistry is also significantly altered. The most notable effect of PTSD on brain chemistry is an increase in cortisol and norepinephrine (Bremner, 2006). Both cortisol and norepinephrine are involved in the stress response. Under normal conditions, of course, stress plays an important, often positive, functional role. However, when a person is chronically stressed, as is the case in PTSD, the response is maladaptive.

Schizophrenia

Schizophrenia is a disorder typically characterized by delusions and hallucinations, often augmented, as well, with motor disturbances. It is estimated that 1% of all individuals have schizophrenia. Because schizophrenia appears to be a disorder that truly resides within the brain and seems to be far less impacted by counseling approaches, many researchers have attempted to understand this disorder from a neurobiological perspective.

Case of Henry

Henry had been on Risperdal for years. He had been in a state hospital for over 30 years under treatment for schizophrenia. With the state hospitals all closing down, he had been released several months ago to the care of an adult group home. Still on his Risperdal, he was numbed and medicated to a state that more closely mirrored a zombie than a functioning human being. His clothing and appearance were typically in tatters, and he usually had left his fly open, which would be noticed only after one observed the large amount of drool on the front of his shirt. The amount of Risperdal was meant to help Henry with his schizophrenic thoughts as well as his potential for violence. One effect noticed by all who knew Henry was that he struggled to speak clearly, sounding "drunk." One day, in fact, his counselor saw a very different presentation by Henry.

Henry: Hey doc (*he said in a crystal-clear voice*).

Doc: Hi Henry, wow, you look sharp today.

Henry: Yeah, I thought you might notice.

Doc: What gives?

Henry: Well doc. I found a dealer on the corner where I live, and I got some crack. I feel real good.

Hallucinations and delusions common to most schizophrenics are believed to be caused by an excess of dopamine (DA) in the brain. Medications used to treat schizophrenia, such as Risperdal, work by affecting DA activity in the brain. Risperdal and other antipsychotic drugs do not directly decrease brain DA levels, but instead block the receptors in the brain to which DA binds, thus rendering DA ineffective. The effect of antipsychotic medication is that the patient typically experiences fewer—and less severe—hallucinations and delusions. For some individuals, DA antagonists completely prevent the psychotic symptoms associated with schizophrenia.

Of course, this information suggests strongly that perhaps the most important aspect to an effective treatment regimen for individuals diagnosed with schizophrenia is that they remain on their meds regularly. Failure to adhere to the prescribed dosage will quickly allow the chemical imbalance in the brain to recharge and increase both the severity and amount of hallucinations.

Although antipsychotics are effective at treating the "disorders of thought" associated with schizophrenia, they are not without side effects. Individuals who take antipsychotics report symptoms consistent with what Doc observed in Henry—increased saliva, fatigue, and drowsiness. Not surprisingly, some drugs of abuse that produce schizophrenic-like behaviors (i.e., cocaine) increase brain DA levels. These unwanted side effects of antipsychotic medications occur because they attenuate DA activity generally. In other words, antipsychotics reduce DA activity not only in the parts of the brain responsible for producing hallucinations and delusions, but also parts of the brain that need DA to produce "normal" behavior—motor behavior. Parkinson's disease is a disorder caused by the death of DA neurons in the brain and is characterized by motor impairments. Schizophrenics exhibit motor dysfunction (fatigue, difficulty speaking, drooling) because DA is altered in the motor regions as well as the psychotic regions.

It is interesting, but not surprising, that Henry's overt behavior appeared normal when he was under the influence of crack cocaine. Cocaine, in general, affects DA levels in the brain, so the crack cocaine enabled Henry to have increased motor control of his body and look more "put together." It essentially counteracted the effect of his Risperdal. The obvious lesson here, of course, is that clinicians working with schizophrenics need to be in regular contact with both the client and her/his prescribing physician in order to monitor the ongoing effectiveness and utility of the medications being prescribed.

Following along the line of research that suggests that schizophrenia is a condition of the brain caused by excessive DA, researchers have investigated the use of many types of medications to positively influence clients while decreasing side effects. Using PET scanning, Arakawa et al. (2010) investigated the impact of Perospirone on dopamine receptors. They found that, in fact, clients may respond well to this medication and that the blockage of a significant number of dopamine receptors seems to result in decreased audio and visual hallucinations.

One of the major risk factors for many clients diagnosed with schizophrenia is polydipsia. This condition occurs in a considerable percentage of clients with schizophrenia and results in clients ingesting unhealthy amounts of water (De Carolis et al., 2010). Researchers have suggested that this form of schizophrenia is associated not only with dopamine receptors, but also orexin receptors and genetic polymorphism (Meerabux et al., 2005).

Counselors need to recognize that the use of medications for clients diagnosed with schizophrenia is critical. Additionally, client care includes medical checkups to monitor (ensure) the client's progress; these need to be regularly scheduled and *kept*.

ADHD

ADHD is a disorder that affects millions of children. It is unknown why more than twice as many boys than girls are affected by ADHD. Although it is still poorly understood, increasing evidence suggests that several brain regions are involved, one of which is the cerebellum. Compared to normal children, the cerebellum of children with ADHD is generally smaller in size (O'Halloran, Kinsella, & Storey, 2011).

Case of Ted

Ted has always been an energetic young boy. By the age of four, his parents noticed, as did others who knew him, that he was different in this way. Now, at the age of seven, he continues to act out, displays little control, and appears to be extremely active for his age. He has been seeing the school counselor for two years now. They engage in play therapy at least twice a week.

Several reports suggest that cerebral glucose metabolism is significantly reduced throughout the brain in ADHD individuals. In the brain, glucose metabolism is an index of brain activity. Since glucose supplies cells with energy to function, when glucose metabolism is elevated in a particular brain region, it is generally because that structure has been very active. Zametkin et al. (1999) found that adults diagnosed with ADHD as children exhibited depressed cerebral glucose metabolism, with the most prominent effects occurring in the prefrontal cortex (PFC) and premotor cortex (PMC). Reduced cerebral glucose metabolism in the frontal lobes has also been found in adolescent girls with ADHD (Ernst et al., 1994; Zametkin et al., 1993; Ernst, 1997). Interestingly, these results do not generalize to adolescent boys (Ernst et al., 1994; Ernst et al., 1997). Nonetheless, that evidence suggests a link between reduced frontal lobe activity and ADHD is significant, given that the frontal lobes are associated with "executive" functions—behaviors that are involved in attention and planning, for example.

Stimulants are typically prescribed to individuals with ADHD to counteract their hypoactive brain activity. The idea is that stimulants, such as Ritalin, may increase the brain's activity so that it is comparable to the activity of a normal brain. By increasing PFC and PMC activity, executive functions are enhanced and behavior is "normalized." Lou et al. (1984; 1989; 1990) found that with stimulant medication, brain perfusion increased.

Drugs and Alcohol

Case of Cliff

Cliff had been using marijuana for years. He liked the way it made the rest of his life seem manageable. His friends all smoked pot as well. As the years went by, from high school into college and several years after, he noticed that his friends had all graduated from college and worked their way into good jobs, and some had even started having families. Cliff had none of those things. He had become so engulfed by the joy and pleasure, and by this point the need to use marijuana, that he had lost track of goals and dreams he once had. Sitting next to him in group was Merle. Merle had been a drinker for over twenty years. He started with beer and progressed to bottles of whiskey. The two men, though having chosen different types of drugs, were now in the process of getting sober and trying to maintain their sobriety.

Counselor: Why don't we hear from Merle. Merle, can you tell us about how you realized it was time to try to stop using?
Merle: I had run out of money, had lost my family, and really I had all but destroyed my life. I had been told years before that I needed to get sober, but I thought everyone was just trying

to control me. Funny thing though, it was the booze that was controlling me.

Cliff: (*nodding in agreement*) I hear that. I mean, I now know what people mean when they say they hit their rock bottom. I was begging all of my friends for a few bucks to get high. Suddenly, it hit me that I was in trouble. But, I still didn't stop. A few weeks after that, I got stopped by the cops while driving my friend's minivan. I was high as a kite. (*looking down in shame*) I mean, I didn't even know where I was. The judge sentenced me to drug court, I went through detox, and then after four or five relapses, I am here 45 days sober.

Although the preferred drug of choice is different for Cliff and Merle, the brain of each is probably very similar. All addicts, at one time in their lives, made a conscious decision to use the substance to which they are addicted. So why not simply stop using? The reason is that drugs cause changes in the brain that prevent an addict from being able—both mentally and physically—to stop the use of the substance. These changes include alterations in brain chemistry along with hardwired physical changes.

One primary and exceedingly significant change in the brains of those under the influence of drugs of abuse is that DA levels are significantly elevated. This excess DA contributes to the feeling of euphoria often associated with the use of drugs and alcohol because the neurotransmitter affects brain regions involved during activities most people find pleasurable. The effect of DA is so rewarding that animals will not only self-administer drugs intravenously to receive a "high," but they will also self-administer electrical stimulation to the brain regions that receive DA input!

Like a thermostat, the human brain is equipped to regulate itself. When the brain's chemistry is altered, the brain responds by altering itself in an attempt to maintain homeostasis. When one uses drugs, the brain responds in many ways, one of which is to produce tolerance to the excess DA. The brain may increase the level of enzymes that break down DA and render it ineffective.

In addition to the neurochemical changes that occur following drug use, the brain also undergoes structural changes. Addiction to drugs and alcohol is believed by many to be a form of learning that is mediated by synaptic changes. When one is addicted, the brain's circuitry literally becomes wired differently, and in order to treat addiction, the circuitry must be rewired.

Clients who stop using after lengthy use of a drug will probably go through what is called withdrawal. Whether the clients try to stop on their own or through the use of a detoxification center, there will be significant and traumatic effects on the body (Brooks & McHenry, 2009). Side effects from withdrawal vary depending on several factors including the drug of choice, amount, tolerance, and length of time used. However, the violent shock to the system goes beyond sweats, nausea, vomiting, and agitation. Within the brain and central nervous system (CNS), as the chemical leaves the system, failure to readjust the system, brain, and CNS may result in what is called "dry drunk" (Brooks & McHenry, 2009). This condition occurs when the clients actually have stopped the use of the substance but continue the old patterns and styles of living they maintained when they were using. Ultimately, many recovering addicts must relearn how to live life. In recovering, they must learn not only how to live without the substance and its effects, but also how to live with their "new brain." Unfortunately, the rewiring that occurred while under the influence can, in some cases, continue even after the drug is stopped.

Cutting

Self-mutilation is a fairly prevalent issue in our society, with estimates of 12% of the general population and up to 20% of the psychiatric population engaging in such behavior (Favazza, De-Rosear, & Conterio, 1989). A particularly prevalent form of self-mutilation is cutting. The act of cutting appears to underlie a more serious psychological problem since individuals who cut also tend to have co-diagnoses such as depression and anxiety (Andover et al., 2005), eating disorders (Favazza, DeRosear, & Conterio, 1989), and borderline personality disorder (Suyemoto, 1998).

So why do people cut? What does the act of self-mutilation provide to depressed, anxious, and psychiatric patients? One theory suggests that cutting is a way in which individuals physically express pain they are unable to verbalize. Interestingly, however, people who cut report feeling a tremendous amount of guilt and disgust after they perform the self-injurious act. So why do people then *continue* to cut? A recent study suggests that cutters may have abnormally low levels of beta-endorphins, chemicals in the brain that act as natural painkillers by binding to opioid receptors (Stanley et al., 2010). As with many drugs that are abused, when endorphins bind to opioid receptors, one experiences feelings of euphoria. Consequently, during the act of self-injurious behavior, brain chemicals that produce pleasure reward and reinforce that behavior, thereby increasing the likelihood that the behaviors will be repeated. If people continue to cut themselves because the pain associated with cutting increases endorphins and produces pleasure, then might the creation of interference in that cycle stop the behavior? The research is equivocal. While some research suggests that using certain drugs that block endorphins from binding to opioid receptors does result in less self-injurious behavior in humans (Herman et al., 2004; Kars et al., 1990; Symons, Thompson, & Rodriguez, 2004), other studies do not (Szymanski et al., 1987; Willemsen-Swinkels et al., 1995). These disparate findings then suggest that cutting may not be simply a biologically mediated behavior and that psychological factors are probably also very much involved.

Case of Suzie

Suzie is a polite, caring, and respectful young woman. She has arrived at the college counseling center because of "concerns" she has about herself and life. Adding little more during the intake process, she schedules a visit with one of the counselors. Tom has been at the counseling center for several years and has seen many different types of clients. By the third session, the counselor and client were communicating clearly about her issues and concerns. Most were developmentally appropriate issues related to being away at college, relationships with peers, and finding her place in the world. Then, in the middle of the fifth session, Suzie disclosed something new.

Suzie: (*as she was running her hands up and down the tops of her legs*) I wanted to tell you about something I do that I am not very proud of.

Tom: OK, I can see this is difficult for you. Continue when you are ready.

Suzie: Well, (*pointing to her legs*) I cut myself.

Tom: You mean that you injured yourself, or are you talking about actually purposefully cutting yourself on a regular basis?

Suzie: I mean, I don't do it every day or anything, but, yeah, I cut the tops of my legs probably once or twice a week.

Conclusion

Mental health issues that clients present with in counseling can be understood from both a counseling theory/approach (Rational Emotive Behavior Therapy, Adlerian, Gestalt, etc.), as well as a neurobiological point of view. Accessing and referencing the possible current condition of the brain of the client, as related to his or her mental health issue(s), can have a profound impact on the overall analysis of the case as well as the approach(es) used by the counselor to most effectively, efficiently, and positively affect the client.

As our field continues to refine its approaches through the use of effective and useful neurobiological information, increasingly effective counseling remedies will emerge. However, until that time arrives, we suggest that counselors combine their current counseling approaches with best practices that target the possible problem areas of the brain (both structural and chemical) as a means to help clients with their mental health conditions.

Chapter Review Questions

1. How does neurobiology account for the "sister" disorders of anxiety and depression residing in the same parts of the brain?
2. In considering the mental health condition of schizophrenia, what does the current neurocounseling perspective suggest is the most useful therapeutic approach?
3. While schizophrenia seems to be an extreme amount of dopamine entering the brain, which other condition discussed in this chapter is the result of the client's apparent need/want for more and more dopamine?

6

PSYCHOTROPIC MEDICATIONS

With the increased availability and utility of medications that have positive effects on the brain chemistry of clients, counselors need to be aware of both the general and sometimes specific medications being used. Since all such psychotropic medications have some degree of impact on chemical levels in the brain, they often influence the client's mood, thoughts, and/or feelings, causing changes in client behaviors. Because the goals of counseling are also targeted at thoughts, feelings, and behaviors, every effort should be made to ensure that both types of interventions are complimentary and growth fostering.

To that end, allow us a moment to discuss how different worldviews might have impact on either the effective or ineffective use of medications in the counseling process.

Before we describe and delineate the various and varied medications prescribed to help clients cope with mental health issues, it is first imperative that we address the different worldviews involved in the effective and ineffective use of medications in the counseling process.

Your Worldview and Medications

While counselors do not prescribe medications, you are typically in a position where you can have some effect on the *client's* decisions regarding their use. Thus, you have a responsibility for understanding the reasons medications are being used and their possible side effects. Beyond those basics, however, we believe it is very important that you have a clear grasp of your own view regarding their use. Counselor attitudes here run the entire gamut of possibilities. Some counselors have shared with us the belief that medications are often simply prescribed as a crutch and hold no real potential in effecting the necessary changes that may be needed for the client to obtain any real long-term relief from psychological distress. In essence, they believe that medications are useless at best and actually counterproductive at worst because they simply mask the basic underlying psychological issues that should be being addressed in the counseling process. On the other end of the continuum are those counselors who believe that there needs to be even more emphasis on prescribing medications to clients. They often base their thesis on positive client changes and long-term positive impacts they have witnessed, which they attribute to the *combination* of medication use and the counseling process.

Certainly, it should be clearly noted here that the *ultimate decision* as to whether or not to take medications for psychological reasons is *solely that of the client in conjunction with his or her prescribing doctor.* Nevertheless, it is important that you think through your own attitude on this matter. You should recognize that even if you try to ignore this issue, your own biases and prejudices regarding their use might become evident during the counseling process. You will be asked what you think of medications. You will be asked for ideas regarding which medications work best for certain issues. Be prepared.

To help in that preparation, this chapter includes information about not only which medications are typically prescribed for varied types of psychological distress, but also the latest information the field has regarding how these medications affect the chemistry of the brain. Please clearly note here that the vast majority of medical doctors, psychiatrists, and pharmaceutical companies understand that *all* prescribed medications are simply "best guesses." This is certainly not to suggest that prescriptions are haphazardly doled out by the uninformed, but rather that the drug, dosage, and duration are not established certainties, and that there is a need to carefully and continually monitor, assess, and reassess how the medication is affecting each particular client. Each individual will respond in a somewhat different way to each different type of medication prescribed; hence, a counselor who is well informed about medications can really help a client optimize the positive results of the client's medical regimen. Although over half of the people in America are on some type of prescribed medication (for physical, cognitive, and/or psychological issues), clients will respond to the idea of being on medications for mental health issues in many different ways. In this regard, we see a parallel process to that found in both family systems theory as well as multicultural counseling processes. By this we mean that clients may often arrive at the decision regarding the use or nonuse of medications through beliefs they have learned through culture, family system rules, and, of course, their own devices. Variables here include the type of medication being considered, whether or not the client has ever been on psychotropics, and the expected duration of the medication regimen. Simply put, the use of psychotropics is a personal decision anchored in a variety of different pieces of information available to the client.

Case of Juanita

I (Bill) worked with a client who over the course of two sessions described both herself and every person in her immediate family as suffering from mental health issues. She had been to see numerous counselors, psychologists, and psychiatrists who had tried to "remove" or "cure" her depression. None of their attempts seemed to have had long-lasting results. Once I understood that in her world she would not accept being "without a condition," I was able to reframe her case as one of learning to live and cope effectively with her depression. I told her she would always have a degree of depression. She agreed and we worked on not only her cognitive and behavioral responses to mood, but also discussed her use of medications. She had been on antidepressants for years. Under her doctor's care, she took a medication "holiday." Basically, she came off her medications. Over time, she came to the decision that the medications were having a negative impact on her and that she was better off without taking the meds. We worked for a while on her skills in coping with depression and her attitude, self-concept, view of the world, and affect all improved dramatically.

Questions: How might the use of medications have been clouding her view of things? Knowing that she would not give up the term depression to describe herself, how important was it to evaluate both the frame she chose as well as the use of medications?

Advocacy

No matter what personal view you hold regarding the use of medications, it is important that you help your client advocate for self as well as understand the impacts, both positive and negative, associated with the use of psychotropics. Of course, as counselors, we must understand that a multitude of different variables influence the way that medications affect a client. As a counselor, it is important to recognize your role is in helping clients assess these variables. Some general things to consider along with the medication (including dose) include age, weight, previous medical issues, genetic predispositions to medications, lifestyle issues (exercise, diet, drinking, smoking, etc.), and current life stressors. In relation to clients and their use of medications, part of the role of a professional counselor is to promote active and honest discussions with the clients about their use of medications as well as the effects (both positive and negative).

Who Is Prescribing the Medications?

The field of counseling, of course, does not exist in a vacuum. In some states, licensed professional counselors (LPCs) are unable to diagnose and must rely on psychologists, psychiatrists, or medical doctors to document and provide diagnostic terminology for third-party reimbursement. In all states, medications can only be prescribed by licensed physicians (including, of course, psychiatrists). As many counselors will attest to, the range in knowledge regarding psychological issues and associated diagnoses can vary greatly when we consider the prescribing practices of general practitioners.

If you go to a doctor today, chances are, if there is a real concern, you will be referred to a specialist. This is typically because there is so much information on any one aspect of the human body that a general practitioner cannot possibly be fully knowledgeable about all of it (e.g., heart conditions, arthritis, etc.). However, when it comes to diagnosing and prescribing medications for psychological issues and conditions, general practitioners are still in the position of (in many cases) making type, dosage, and duration decisions often based on limited information. We do not assert, as others might in our field, that general practitioners should not be prescribing psychotropics. We do feel, however, that part of the role of professional counselors is to help the client assess the diagnostic fit and prescribed substances.

In some cases, clients may benefit from suggestions on the part of the counselor to consider discussing with their doctor the possibility of incorporating medications into their treatment protocol. This is certainly not meant to suggest in any way that we condone the practice of counselors coercing clients into the use of medications, but rather, we are suggesting that frank and open discussions, when called for, can normalize the process highlighting both positive impacts and side effects of psychotropic medications. In these instances, a well-informed counselor who can articulate clearly to a client how different classifications of medications work may well increase the chance of success on both ends—counseling *and* medication.

What the Medications Actually Do

Truth be known, we still do not know exactly and definitively what psychotropic medications do to the brains of clients. Most research findings are replete with indefinite phrases such as "the medication might . . ." or "it appears that perhaps there is a connection between the use of this medication and . . . effects." While these statements may appear vague, they are accurate, based as they are on our present knowledge of how the drug works. There are very few real absolutes in life. That being the case, often, especially with psychotropics that have been on the market for a while, we (as a field) accept and believe (usually based on *some* measures of empirical data) that medication A has the greatest potential for positively affecting a client with issue A.

Counselors who garner information and clarity on the ways that meds work—not just tangentially and broadly (e.g., "This medication is used for mood disorders and should help your depression."), but with some degree of specificity (e.g., "This medication is an SSRI. It will most likely help balance the amount of serotonin in your brain. This balance will in turn possibly help elevate your mood.")—all other things being equal, will probably be better able to help their clients. The difference between these two statements is simple yet profound regarding the clarity and purpose of consulting with clients who are either on or considering taking psychotropic medications.

Combining your increasingly deeper understanding of the ways that medications work with your already vested knowledge in the general and specific parts of the brain that may become problematic when certain psychological issues are present (remember chapter 2), the following information will expand your worldview on what psychological distress looks like from the inside out. As counselors, we are typically quite adept at understanding what depression looks like in the typical client or how a client with generalized anxiety disorder presents. We have talked with these clients and know their typical patterns. Coupling an understanding of both the structural and chemical basis for various client issues with the ways medications for typical psychological conditions work will further enable you to more fully grasp the totality of the client and her or his concerns and challenges.

We finish this section with a consideration of the use of "will power" in dealing with psychological concerns. It is certainly clear that resiliency, will to thrive, and the inherent desire of all people to lead a balanced and harmonious life are present in our clients. However, while these traits can play important roles, as such, in helping clients improve, in many cases, will power alone may not be sufficient. Often, no one aspect, *in and of itself,* is sufficient. In fact, this may be why many research studies that look at medications alone versus therapy alone versus the combination of therapy and medication find that combination usually affects the greatest positive impact on the client's well-being. And is not such improvement our primary goal as counselors? Being armed and prepared with useful information on the brain will allow you to better converse with clients on medications as well as clarify that in many cases, even though willpower may help in the process of getting better, it may also be the *chemistry of the client's brain* that needs to be changed.

Classifications of Psychotropic Medications

There exists a multitude of different types of medications prescribed and taken for different types of mental health issues. Some have what are considered minor side effects, while others can have quite adverse and strong physical and/or psychological impacts. Counselors are not medical doctors, nor are we psychiatrists; we do not write prescriptions. However, the more familiar you become with commonly prescribed meds, the better equipped you will be at conversing with clients regarding the utility of taking such meds.

The purpose of the remainder of this chapter is to introduce you to several different classifications of medications along with their hypothesized effects on the brain. The major categories of medications addressed are *SSRIs, SNRIs, tricyclics, MAOIs, mood stabilizers, antipsychotics, and stimulants commonly used in treating mental health issues.* All psychotropic drugs change neurotransmitter levels in the brain. In fact, all drugs—legal or illicit, prescribed or not—affect chemicals in the brain by altering the rate at which they are made, by modifying their release and breakdown, or by mimicking the chemical and binding to its receptors. All of these actions result in either an increase or decrease in neurotransmitter levels, restoring the brain to a more balanced state.

Serotonin-Based Medications

Serotonin, or the lack thereof, has been hypothesized to play a role in depression since 1967 (Coppen, 1967). Serotonin affects mood, sleep, appetite, emotion, and sexual appetite (Nelson et al., 1997). Because serotonin dysregulation is considered one of the primary issues that contribute to depression, drugs that enhance brain serotonin levels are widely used in the treatment of the disorder.

SSRIs

Selective serotonin reuptake inhibitors (SSRIs) are commonly used to treat disorders associated with low levels of serotonin, such as depression, anxiety, and OCD. SSRIs were first used in the United States in 1988 (fluoxetine) and work by preventing extracellular serotonin from being reabsorbed by the cell from which it is released. This reuptake inhibition thereby allows more of the neurotransmitter to be available to bind with postsynaptic receptors (Ferguson, 2001). Figure 6.1 illustrates how SSRIs work to enhance the efficacy of serotonin. Under normal conditions, serotonin is released from the presynaptic terminal of the axon into the synaptic cleft where it binds to serotonin receptors on the dendrites of the postsynaptic cell as well as reuptake sites on the presynaptic terminal. SSRIs block the reuptake sites, forcing

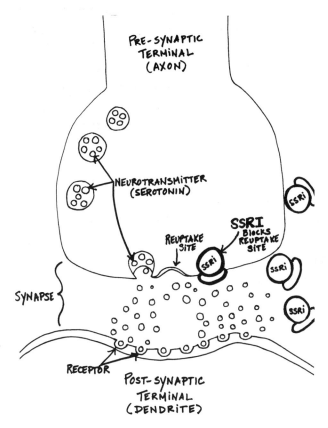

Figure 6.1 **SSRIs enhance serotonin in the brain by blocking serotonin reuptake sites on the presynaptic terminal.**

serotonin to be maintained within the synapse, which ultimately increases its effect on the postsynaptic cell.

This classification of medications is used to help restore a more natural balance to the brain chemistry by targeting serotonin levels. In a "normal" brain, adequate serotonin is released from one cell to exert an effect on another cell. The serotonin that is not used is either taken back by the cell that released it, or dissolved by enzymes—both processes are necessary to maintain balance in the "normal" brain. Since it is believed that depression may be due to too little serotonin, one way to enhance the effect of what serotonin one has, is to allow it to remain active for a longer period of time. SSRIs do this by preventing the serotonin in the synaptic cleft from being removed.

SSRIs are typically prescribed for clients with depression. However, some clients with anxiety-based conditions also respond well to this classification of medications. Additional psychological conditions that seem to be positively affected by SSRIs are *panic disorders, OCD, and PTSD* (Bank, 2012).

As with each medication, there are side effects. The common concerns cited by clients in taking SSRIs are unpleasant effects such as nausea, sedation, insomnia, dizziness, sexual dysfunction, and decreased appetite (Bank, 2012). In addition, this classification of medications, because of the chemical impact it has on the brain, takes time to actually begin to show results. In many cases, it takes three to four weeks before the client experiences some

Table 6.1 **Common SSRIs**

Medication	Generic
Celexa	Citalopram
Luvox	Fluvoxamine
Paxil	Paroxetine
Prozac	Fluoxetine
Zoloft	Sertraline
Lexapro	Escitalopram

degree of relief. Because of the delayed gratification of SSRIs on behavior, many patients discontinue their use before benefits are derived. Therefore, as a counselor, it is imperative that we are able to discuss both the impact these medications are having on the client's brain and why it takes a while to kick in, and it is also imperative to educate the client on the need to assess for both the positive impacts as well as negative effects they experience in using these psychotropics. Additionally, it is imperative that we counsel the client not to stop taking the medication until he/she has consulted with his/her doctor.

Case of Johnny

Johnny has been taking an SSRI for three months. His doctor told him that it would take some time before the medication starts to really influence his mood. The dosage and regimen for taking his medication has not changed since he was initially prescribed the medication. He has been depressed for two years over the death of his fiancé. He asks you point-blank, "Should I keep taking these medications? All they do is make me sleepy."

What are some things you could share with Johnny about the SSRI he is taking, as well as its performance?

SNRIs

Selective norepinephrine reuptake inhibitors (SNRIs) are similar to SSRIs in that they work to enhance certain chemicals in the brain. However, whereas SSRIs block only serotonin reuptake sites, SNRIs target both serotonin and norepinephrine reuptake sites. The end result of SNRIs is to increase the binding of both serotonin and norepinephrine to the postsynaptic cell by blocking their reuptake by the presynaptic cell. This classification of

Table 6.2 **Common SNRIs**

Medication	Generic
Cymbalta	Duloxetine
Effexor	Venlafaxine

medications is typically used to treat depression, anxiety disorders, and social phobias.

Tricyclics

Tricyclic antidepressants (TCAs) are the oldest class of antidepressant medications. Imipramine, the first TCA used specifically for the treatment of depression, was developed in the 1950s (Kuhn, 1958). TCAs are named for their three-ring molecular structure. Like SSRIs and SNRIs, TCAs are believed to exert their antidepressant effects by preventing the reuptake of serotonin and norepinephrine. Although very effective, TCAs are less selective than their newer counterparts and also tend to produce more severe side effects. As such, they are less commonly used today and tend to be the drug of choice only when the others have not been effective.

Table 6.3 **Common Tricyclics**

Medication	Generic
Tofranil	Imipramine
Elavil	Amitriptyline
Norpramin	Desipramine
Sinequan	Doxepin
Surmontil	Trimipramine
Vivactil	Protriptyline
Anafranil	Clomipramine
Pamelor	Nortriptyline

MAOIs

Along with tricyclics, monoamine oxidase inhibitors (MAOIs) have been used to treat psychological conditions (especially depression) for years. However, due to the fact that the side effects of either SNRIs or SSRIs are typically far less severe than MAOIs, many prescribing doctors favor the use of SSRIs and SNRIs over MAOIs. MAOIs are most often prescribed today as a last effort to treat depressed clients with medications.

MAOIs interfere with the breakdown of monoamine transmitters. Most MAOIs are not selective in which transmitters they affect (which is what can make them have serious side effects). It is thought that MAOIs have an impact on levels of serotonin, melatonin, epinephrine, and norepinephrine. In this way, we might consider the use of this medication to be similar to that of a shotgun approach. Because this is an older form of medicating depression, it served as a first-generation drug class. The SSRIs and SNRIs are far more selective (more of a rifle than shotgun) and thus have less unintended side effects on the overall chemistry of the brain.

Side effects for MAOIs are typically more serious than other meds used for depression and anxiety and include the possibility of stroke, heart attack, and death if taken along with substances containing the chemical tyramine. Tyramine is found in other medications as well as foods such as wine, cheese, and pickles.

Table 6.4 **Common MAOIs**

Medication	Generic
Marplan	Isocarboxazid
Nardil	Phenelzine
Parnate	Tranylcypromine

Mood Stabilizers

The varied classes of medications just covered fall under the umbrella of medications for *mood disorders*. Mood stabilizers are a very different type of medication classification that treats conditions associated with psychology conditions such as bipolar disorder, aggression, and impulsivity (not to be confused with symptoms of ADHD). Many of the medications found in this class can have severe side effects and warrant regular blood monitoring to check the levels of the medication in the client's system.

LITHIUM-BASED

Lithium-based medications associated with mood stabilization target neurotransmitters that regulate mood. The primary neurotransmitters that these meds influence control the amount of serotonin and dopamine in the brain. In essence, just as SSRIs control the amount of serotonin reuptake, lithium-based meds act in a way that blocks intake of too much dopamine and yet also allows an increased amount of serotonin to be utilized by the brain.

ANTICONVULSANTS

Although lithium is considered by many to be the primary drug of choice for clients with severe mood swings (manic and depressive), in recent years, several different medications originally designed to treat seizure disorders have shown promising effects on clients with bipolar disorder. Just as different types of medications work differently for clients with depression, so too do

Table 6.5 **Common Lithium-Based Mood Stabilizers**

Medication	Generic
Eskalith, Eskalith-CR, Lithane, Lithobid, Lithonate, Lithotabs	Lithium Carbonate

Table 6.6 Common Anticonvulsants Used for Mood Stabilization

Medication	Generic
Depakote	Valproic Acid
Lamictal	Lamotrigine
Tegretol	Carbamazepine
Trileptal	Oxcarbazepine

we find that some clients respond to lithium-based meds while others respond more positively to the antiseizure meds in this classification category.

Antipsychotics

Overall, perhaps the most challenging cases that a counselor works with are those clients who suffer from severe mental illness described best as *psychosis*. Although a number of DSM diagnoses fit this description, the general rule of thumb includes some degree of living in a world that really does not exist. Whether it is audio hallucinations, visual hallucinations, and/or in combination with extreme feelings of paranoia, homicidal ideation, or extreme cases of Axis II personality disorders, these clients appear to have significant chemical and/or structural issues in their brains.

The primary challenge is that there really is no known cure for these types of conditions. Rather, there is maintenance of the symptoms and counseling the client to lead as normal and productive of a life as possible. Although numerous causes have been cited for the development of psychosis (e.g., genetics, abuse, head trauma, etc.), one of the keys in helping these clients is to understand not only the medications available, but as with other psychotropics, and perhaps even more specific to this classification of drugs, the significant side effects that can result.

The primary hypothesis for this classification of drugs is that psychosis forms as a result of overactive dopamine receptors. This overactivity in turn results in the formation of delusional thinking and/or audio/visual hallucinations. By blocking the dopamine receptors, many medications in this classification limit the frequency, duration, and severity of such thoughts.

As with other types of medications, the onset of symptom relief can vary from client to client. However, the majority of clients see marked diminishment in their agitation and hallucinations within days of starting medications. Typically, it takes six to eight weeks for clients to see significant changes in their thought patterns. This is important because there are typically two points during which clients will stop taking their medications (usually either during the initial few days/weeks *or* after they have had significant symptom relief for several months and start to believe they no longer need the medications).

The side effects of this classification of medications, as mentioned earlier, can be quite severe. Along with typical side effects such as drowsiness, blurred vision, and sensitivity to sun, this classification of medications can cause rigidity in the muscles, muscle spasms, and severe restlessness. Perhaps the most concerning side effect that has been researched and found to be present in approximately 5% of the population who take antipsychotics is a condition called tardive dyskinesia (TD). TD results in mild to severe uncontrollable muscle movements around the

Table 6.7 Common Antipsychotics

Medication	Generic
Haldol	Haloperidol
Loxitane	Loxapine
Moban	Molindome
Navane	Thiothixene
Stelazine	Trifluoperazine
Thorazine	Chlorpromazine

Table 6.8 **Common Atypical Antipsychotics**

Medication	Generic
Abilify	Aripiprazole
Risperdal	Risperidone
Seroquel	Quetiapine
Zyprexa	Olanzapine

mouth. Although some clients can recover after being taken off the medications, some never fully recover from these significant tremors. There are newer (atypical) antipsychotics that seem to cause far fewer cases of TD. These atypical antipsychotics do, however, increase the risk of diabetes, obesity, and high cholesterol. Clients on these meds (below) need to have their blood levels checked regularly while on the medication.

Anti-anxiety Medications

In addition to antidepressants, there are several other types of medications used in conjunction with long-term medications for quick effects. These two classifications are beta-blockers and benzodiazepines. Both classes of meds have very quick results (sometimes within minutes) and can be used along with antidepressants for moments when the anxiety may be at a peak or the client may be in a severely debilitating situation (e.g., a client suffering from severe test anxiety may take Klonopin [a benzodiazepine] prior to a major exam).

However, medications in the benzodiazepine class (Benzos) can lead to addiction. In the event that a client is taking increasingly high amounts of the Benzos, consideration should be given to increasing the amount/dosage of the base antidepressant.

Beta-blockers, such as Inderal, can be used in conjunction with antidepressants to counteract physical symptoms associated with anxiety such as profuse sweating and trembling. This type of

Table 6.9 **Common Benzodiazepines**

Medication	Generic
Ativan	Lorazepam
Klonopin	Clonazepam
Xanax	Alprazolam

medication is typically prescribed for individuals with heart conditions, but when used by clients with anxiety issues can actually mitigate against severe physical manifestations of the anxiety.

Stimulants

Regardless of whether the client is a child, teen, or adult, the primary classification of medication utilized in the treatment of attention deficit and hyperactivity include medications that fall under the category of stimulants. It may appear paradoxical in nature, but the stimulation of certain parts of the brain actually helps focus others. For example, one of the primary hypotheses of what happens in the brain of an individual with ADHD is that the increased compulsivity is related to less control of the cortex of the brain. This is identified through the use of brain imaging that seems to clearly demonstrate decreased activity in the cortex of clients with ADHD. Stimulants actually enhance the activity and firing of the mechanisms in the cortex and thus help the individuals gain more control of their thoughts, behaviors, and feelings.

The primary side effects of stimulants include sleeplessness, decreased appetite, headaches, and stomachaches, and in some cases, tics can develop. Some of the more severe and often much rarer side effects include heart problems, stroke, and increased psychiatric issues such as paranoia, hallucinations, and mania.

Use of Medications

Counselors typically have a group of theoretical positions and therapeutic techniques that they call on when working with clients. Most describe their primary processes of working with clients on their informed consent (e.g., I utilize a counseling approach that is anchored in processes consistent with cognitive-behavioral therapy). Such is the nature of being a professional in any field; you cannot have a strong handle on *every* therapeutic tool—but with practice, you can develop a high degree of skill across several landscapes. We find the same to be true of prescribing doctors. In most cases, doctors prescribe the medications that they have found to be useful for previous clients. This becomes a pattern of prescriptions. Although some have argued that the primary emphasis for such patterns in prescribing medications is based on rewards or good marketing by pharmaceutical companies, we have found that doctors find medications that work and stick with them.

What this means in practice is that physician A is more likely to prescribe a similar antidepressant to his clients who present with symptoms associated with depression. As a counselor, it is important to advocate for your clients and talk with them about how that particular medication is working or not working. Clients respond in very different ways to the same medication. In this regard, we consider our clients in an individual fashion.

Table 6.10 **Common Stimulants**

Medication	Generic
Adderall	Amphetamine
Dexedrine	Dextroamphetamine
Ritalin	Methylphenidate

Self-Medication

There exist a multitude of ways that a client can choose to self-medicate. In some instances, the use of alcohol (especially in excess) combined with psychotropics can enhance their effect. In other cases, using prescribed psychotropics in combination with other pharmacological agents can cause increased responses or effects. Some clients who have struggled with psychological issues for years may lean toward self-medication as the first line of defense—followed by prescribed medications. In some cases, whether through shame, through guilt, or for whatever reason, clients will lie to their prescribing doctor about their current chemical intakes. This can lead to dangerous if not severe consequences (both psychological and physical). Liver damage, kidney damage, and increased risk of heart conditions or stroke are some of the possible outcomes of mixing nonprescribed drugs or alcohol with prescription psychotropics.

Conclusion

As a professional counselor in today's world, it is imperative that we come to fully recognize that clients on medications or in need of psychotropic medications require additional attention on our part. Arming yourself with effective and up-to-date information about medications can be highly useful in both educating and advocating for our clients' best interests. Psychotropics will continue to be a critical part of the treatment regimen for many clients with serious psychological conditions. Needless to say, but truly at the core of the reality, is the fact that the use of medications *do indeed* have a significant (if only temporary) impact on our clients' brain chemistry and/or structure.

Chapter Review Questions

1. What is the primary difference between SSRIs and SNRIs?
2. Being specific, describe the impact that *your* particular world-view on psychotropics can have on clients.
3. Why does the brain of a client with ADHD typically respond fairly well to stimulants?

7

ASSESSMENT OF BRAIN FUNCTION (WITH TOMMIE HUGHES)

There exists a multitude of different formal and informal ways to assess client thought processes, cognitive impairments, and over-/underfunctioning of parts of the brain. For years, counselors have used instruments, batteries, and informal clinical judgment to assess the problems and potential directions for counseling with individual clients. This chapter will address not only the formal instruments currently being used by clinicians, doctors, and/or other helping professionals to assess brain function, but also ways that counselors can more specifically understand data from assessment techniques to better understand their clients.

It is imperative that we remind all counselors that multimodal assessment of clinical issues is much preferred over simply taking the results from one instrument and assigning meaning (Hood & Johnson, 2007). This is true of most assessment procedures and absolutely critical in the case of assessing brain function.

Assessment in Counseling—The MSE

Assessment in counseling is a necessary component of working with clients. Initial intake assessment is done for a number of reasons, including diagnosis, treatment planning, and perhaps most importantly to understand the clients and the problem/ issue that brought them to counseling. Fundamental to this first assessment is the clinical interview and mental status exam (MSE). The clinical interview can take many forms and vary in depth and length, depending on the needs of the current client situation. Most will include the basic demographic information and why the person is seeking services, but various elements of history are necessary as well. These may include current and past medical history, family medical history, psychological history, and any relevant elements of personal history (Cohen, Swerdlik, & Sturman, 2013). When considering potential impact of brain functioning, the medical aspects become even more important, as does any history of physical trauma, particularly involving the head.

A particular aspect of the clinical interview is a targeted set of items to focus primarily on how the person is presenting at this time, the MSE. These items include the appearance and behavior of the person during the interview. Also, is the person oriented to person, place, time, and the current situation? Are there problems with memory, thinking, speech, language, mood abnormalities, or disturbance of consciousness? In addition, the person's intellectual functioning is estimated along with level of insight into their own functioning, judgment, and impulsivity regarding behavior and decisions (Zuckerman, 2005). When the MSE is done, with brain function in mind, there will be particular attention to elements of interest, for example memory, speech, thought processes, or motor abnormalities (Cohen, Swerdlik, & Sturman, 2013).

When considering a possible neurological component of client behavior, emotions, or thinking, terms that are often used are *hard signs* and *soft signs.* An example of a hard sign would be an abnormal reflex or actual damage found with neuroimaging. A soft sign is the suggestion of a brain problem such as poor performance on a drawing test or a discrepancy in verbal and nonverbal performance on an intellectual measure (Cohen,

Swerdlik, & Sturman, 2013). Some measures of soft signs will be described now regarding abstracting ability and executive function. Measures of hard signs will be discussed later.

The ability to think abstractly can certainly influence the ability to fully participate in counseling. Assessment of this ability can be done through the clinical interview and MSE, but also with more formal assessment tools. Within the MSE the counselor may ask the client to interpret common proverbs (Gregory, 1999), with the level of abstracting ability determined by the depth of the interpretation. For example, the proverb *the grass is greener on the other side of the fence* is fully interpreted as knowing that in life persons can long for what they do not have by judging themselves against what others have. A more concrete interpretation would be literal, such as "the horses think the other pasture is better." The Proverbs Test is an instrument specifically designed to measure abstraction and has been standardized and normed. Another verbal approach to testing abstraction can be found in the age-appropriate Wechsler intellectual measure with the Similarities subtest. This subtest asks how two objects are alike, such as a pear and a grape. Examples of nonverbal measures include the Object Sorting Test and the Wisconsin Card Sorting Test (Cohen, Swerdlik, & Sturman, 2013).

Executive function instruments measure several key areas critical to the counseling process. How well is the person able to organize and plan? What is the level of cognitive flexibility and ability to control impulses? These abilities are associated with frontal and prefrontal lobes of the brain (Cohen, Swerdlik, & Sturman, 2013). A quick screen for executive function is the clock-drawing test (CDT). This is a drawing test with variations in administration and scoring. One example is to give an instruction to draw the face of a clock showing a particular time. While this is a simple task for most people, persons with various kinds of cognitive impairment may perform poorly. It can be suggestive of cognitive impairment, mental health problems, or visual memory impairment. The trail-making test that is a subtest of the Halstead-Reitan Neuropsychological Battery can also be helpful as part of an assessment of executive function (Cohen, Swerdlik, & Sturman, 2013).

Before we delve further into additional individual instruments used in this process, we want to reiterate the fact that although our field has increased its awareness and skill at detecting problems with brain function, structure and chemistry, there is still much more information to garner before we can arrive at any definitive conclusions of certainty. Having said that, though, we want to encourage counselors to recognize that as a part of the counseling and therapeutic process, we already have many of the necessary tools to form potentially accurate hypotheses about what parts of the brain may be influenced or in fact need to be impacted through the therapeutic process. Let us give you an example.

Case of Charlie

Charlie has been seeing counselors for the last five years (on and off). He has recently been court ordered to work with you on his anger management issues. This was the result of getting in an altercation (his third in six months) while out drinking with some friends. He discloses to you that he uses alcohol three to four nights a week and that drinking helps him sleep. Many of his stories from his past have a general theme of anxiety in them. You see in his case file that several years ago, a counselor had Charlie take Form Y of the State-Trait Anxiety Inventory (STAI). You have him take it again. His score on the State scale is slightly elevated, while on the Trait scale it is very high. From your clinical judgment, his story, and the data from the instrument, you may deduce that he has a significant degree of persistent anxiety (Trait Anxiety). Of course, you would need to rule out depression, but it appears that anxiety may be a core issue in this case. How might this assessment information and knowledge of his case help you pinpoint and

> then perhaps work more effectively with the part of his brain that may be overactive?
>
> When combining the data, it may be that Charlie is suffering from a highly overactive amygdala and/or temporal lobe. If this is the case, that would account for his volatility and perhaps even account for his self-medication with alcohol.

Although the previous case is simplified, it represents how adding the knowledge of the brain with our existing clinical skills, awareness, case conceptualization, and of course formal instruments can shed even more light onto the problem and therefore possible therapeutic directions. In this case, because of the overactive amygdala and/or temporal lobe, one course of action may be to address the apparent anger management issues, but when we consider the function of his brain, it may be that the anger issues are more of a symptom of underactivity in the frontal lobe and perhaps the parietal lobe. Therefore, effective counseling may in fact focus more on Charlie's thought processes (logical sequencing practice) and/or engaging in increased motor activities (e.g., physical exercise).

Tests of Neuro-Function

Neuro-assessment instruments and batteries of instruments have been used in the field of counseling for many years (Drummond & Jones, 2010). It is clear that these instruments are of considerable use in both detecting and assessing discrepancies in the neural and sensorimotor activities of individuals. Many of these instruments include multiple scales to assess brain and body function across multiple areas.

The following table provides several examples of currently used formal assessments that can help counselors detect and assess potential structural issues within the brain. However, it should be noted that as with all instruments and batteries of instruments, before using such tools, counselors must assure compliance with both the test manufacturer's requirements and their respective governing bodies' ethical guidelines for administering and interpreting instruments (e.g., American Counseling Association, 2005).

If, in fact, the counselor had access to the results of one or more of these types of instruments (in Table 7.1), the data retrieved may be quite helpful in the development of a counseling plan as well as techniques and approaches the counselor may choose to use with the particular client.

For example, Susan is a 35-year-old woman who has arrived for counseling services at Agency A with the initial complaint of feeling "odd" and "out of it," and "she keeps forgetting things." She tells the intake specialist that the only major change in her life recently was that she had (approximately six months ago) suffered a miscarriage. The intake specialist notes the following: the client seemed to have trouble articulating her story, and the client appeared to demonstrate little or no affect throughout the session. The intake specialist asks her to take several instruments, including the Ross Information Processing Assessment. Her results on the Ross indicate the following: she is exhibiting deficiencies in memory, organization, and auditory functions of both receiving and sending information. The counselor assigned to her case now meets with her.

Although many therapeutic techniques and theoretical views may apply well to this case, the counselor starts by assessing what, if any, parts of her brain may be exhibiting problematic functioning. Upon investigation of the results and through discussion with the client, it becomes apparent that perhaps the significant loss (miscarriage) may have resulted in the substantial change in her temporal lobe (the part of the brain associated with memory, speech, and emotion). It may be that the overwhelming grief caused the frontal lobe to become much more active to "protect" the client from experiencing the emotions in the temporal lobe. With the diminished function of the temporal lobe to limit

Table 7.1 Common Formal Assessment Tools

Instrument Name	Purpose	Age Range	Administration time	Specific Areas assessed
Bender-Gestalt	Used to help assess neuropsychological impairment	Children and adults	10–30 minutes	Mental confusion, motor control, impulsivity, explosiveness, anxiety, shyness, withdrawal
Halstead-Reitan	Used to help assess brain and nervous system function	15+	6–8 hours	Intelligence, speech, rhythm, perception, categorization, visual functions, language
Kaufman Short Neurological Assessment	Used to assess cognitive functioning	Ages 11–85		Attention, orientation, memory and perceptual skills
Luria-Nebraska	Used to help assess neuropsychological functioning	15+	1½–2½ hours	Motor, rhythm, tactile, vision, speech, writing, reading, arithmetic, memory
Quick Neurological Screening test	Used to assess neurological issues related to learning			Muscle control, motor skills, rhythm, spatial organization, perception, balance
Ross Information Processing Assessment	Used to assess deficits in language or cognitive skills			Memory, spatial orientation, organization, auditory functions and recall of data

the emotion for the client, so too came the loss of other temporal lobe functions such as memory and speech.

A counselor may misinterpret the client's inability to discuss the loss as being resistance or defense mechanisms, when in actuality the client may truly not have access to those parts of her brain right now.

So how might the counselor intervene? One way to help the client more fully learn to cope with the loss and regain her overall stability might be to utilize expressive arts techniques. Whether through music, poetry, art, sand tray, or other techniques, the effect on the brain might include the diminished presence and power of the frontal lobe and perhaps left hemisphere overall, while allowing for increased activity of the right hemisphere that might also increase activity in the temporal lobe. Note here, however, careful consideration of this case would also include ruling out medical issues such as disease and head trauma.

While the instruments noted in the table above have been shown to have merit in assessing current brain function and issues with brain and cognitive limitations, other examples of useful assessment tools can also be used by clinicians to help them collect meaningful and useful data, including instruments that collect data that the client reports.

Self-Report Inventories and Checklists of Neuro-Function

One of the limitations inherent in all self-report instruments is that clients are put in the position of self-describing their symptoms and issues (Hood & Johnson, 2007). In some cases, clients may overstate symptoms, while in others, they may minimize or deny issues (e.g., alcohol-use self-report instruments). Therefore, utilizing the data from these instruments *must* be intertwined with other assessment data (e.g., clinical observations, other report instruments, psychological tests, etc.).

There exists a phenomenal amount of instruments available today that can help detect clinical issues and possible brain

Table 7.2 Common Assessments

Instrument Name	Purpose	Age Range	Administration time	Specific Behavior/s assessed	Brain Regions/Systems
Beck Depression Inventory-II	Used to measure the degree to which the client is experiencing depressive symptoms	13+	5–10 minutes	Depression	Serotonin (low) Noradrenergic (low)
Post-traumatic Stress Diagnostic Scale	Used to assess if a client has PTSD	Adult	5–10 minutes	Traumatic Stress	Serotonergic (high)
Connors Rating Scale	Used to assess the children's behaviors	Children and teens	5 minutes	Compulsivity, hyperactivity, attention-deficit	Noradrenergic (low) Serotonergic
Symptom Checklist 90-Revised	Used to determine if the client has clinically significant psychological issues	13+	10–15 minutes	Obsessive-compulsive, depression, anxiety, hostility, psychosis, somatization	Serotonergic

function, chemistry, and/or structural issues. As shown in the case of Charlie at the start of this chapter, a self-report instrument such as the STAI can provide the counselor with increased awareness of potential brain issues in the client. Examples of other instruments that can help detect significant overactivity or underactivity in the brain of the client are listed in Table 7.2 on page 135.

Brain Scans

Undoubtedly, the most important technological advances in recent years related to assessing brain structures and chemistry have been brain imaging devices. Although most counselors do not have access to such devices on a regular basis, in some cases, clients may have had the opportunity to undergo such tests. Results of such imagery can inform counselors as well as physicians as to the possible underlying physical issues affecting the brain of the client. Additionally, counselors who can understand the ways these machines work and what kinds of results can be obtained are in a much better position to be effective consumers of neurobiological research. Finally, one additional benefit to counselors that garner information and knowledge regarding these advanced assessment tools is that such information is of great value when communicating with clients and/or other professionals about brain-related issues and problems.

Computerized Tomography (CT)

A computerized axial tomography exam offers clinicians and counselors the opportunity to investigate structures of the brain by taking pictures of 2-D slices. This form of brain imaging is a bit older than the MRI technologies now available, but has provided the field of neurobiology with clear images of multiple planes of the brain to compare normally functioning brains to abnormally functioning brains. Further, through advanced computer software programs, these 2-D images may be aligned and stacked

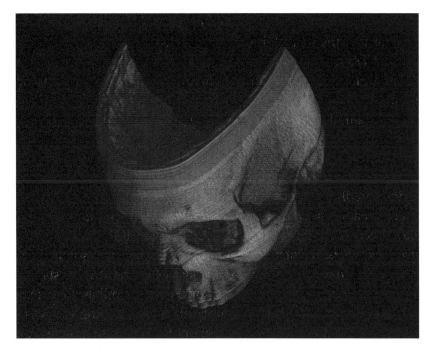

Figure 7.1 **A CT scan of a human skull**

on top of one another to produce fairly clear 3-D-type images for further comparisons. The CT scan is basically a special type of X-ray. Essentially, the brain is X-rayed at many different angles with each providing a different perspective of it. The multiple 2-D X-rays are then combined to provide a holistic, 3-D representation of the specimen. Figure 7.1 is a CT scan of a human skull. The apparent three-dimensionality of the skull was created by superimposing several 2-D X-rays of the object.

Magnetic Resonance Imaging (MRI)

MRI is another common device used to investigate the human body in a noninvasive way. MRI technology is based upon the fact that hydrogen is abundant in all human tissue (Harper, Rodwell, & Mayes, 1977) and that hydrogen atoms, when in the

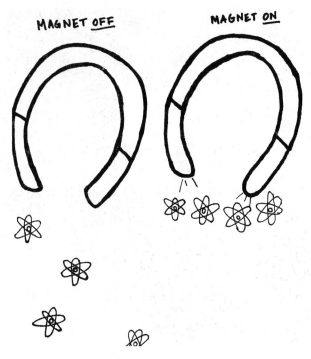

Figure 7.2 **Magnetics are highly utilized in the process of developing MRI scans.**

presence of a magnet, will align themselves with the magnetic force (Figure 7.2). Once the brain's hydrogen atoms have been aligned by the magnet, radio waves are applied to slightly perturb the atoms, which results in an electrical current that is measured and translated into a 3-D color image of the brain. The colors produced by the MRI indicate how active brain regions are, with warmer colors correlating to greater brain activity.

The way an MRI machine works is that it utilizes magnets to send radio waves through the individual's body. These waves are detected at a microscopic level through advanced computer programs. The process in general involves a magnet utilized to align the protons of hydrogen atoms, which when radio waves are added, results in data/images. These computer-derived images can be focused on incredibly small changes in the body.

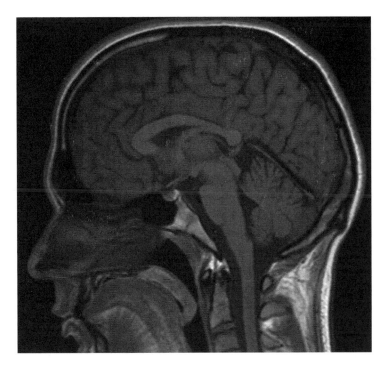

Figure 7.3 **MRI scan of a healthy brain**

Primarily used to distinguish (in either 2-D or 3-D) different types of soft tissue in the brain, such imaging can allow for determinations of small changes in brain tissue over time or detect the size of various structures in the brain. The MRI scan above (Figure 7.3) is of a healthy, adult human brain.

Functional Magnetic Resonance Imaging (fMRI)

Through advancing technologies, the MRI process has evolved to include a much more enhanced and developed set of data that can be obtained from scans. Using a similarly styled machine as an MRI, an fMRI can be used to collect real-time data on the brain versus the snapshot photos provided via MRIs. Because the fMRI machine is highly detailed in its results, along

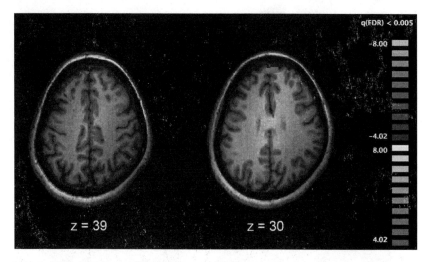

Figure 7.4 fMRI is used to examine brain activity in real time. The brain on the left is a healthy, normal adult. The brain on the right is of a schizophrenic patient. Images were acquired from each participant as they performed a working memory task. The healthy control has more brain activity relative to the schizophrenic.

with large-scale structural images, this device also allows for the viewing of blood/oxygen levels in each part of the brain. This data allows for a much clearer picture in real time of what parts of the brain are active and what parts are inactive.

Positron Emission Tomography (PET)

Like the MRI, PET is another dynamic brain scan that has arrived in recent years that allows us a clearer understanding of the brain function. PET technology measures brain activity by detecting changes in the brain's utilization of oxygen and glucose, the primary energy source of all cells. Prior to being put in the scanner, a small amount of radioactive material is injected into the patient's bloodstream. Because glucose and oxygen are delivered to all cells via the blood, cells that are highly active absorb more radioactive material than cells that are not. Both organs and tissues can be assessed in function and activity through the use of imaging the body after radioactive material has been injected.

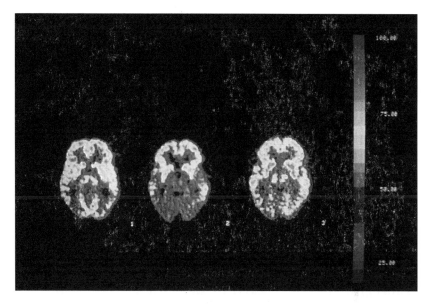

Figure 7.5 **PET scans obtained from a healthy (scan 1) and AIDS patient (scans 2 and 3). Treatment with AZT (scan 3) increased brain activity in the AIDS patient.**

The radioactive material is used because it coagulates in places in the body that are demonstrating high degrees of chemical activity. Therefore, when brain PET scans are used, they produce images of the parts of the brain that are firing the most. These images can also point toward parts of the brain that are dormant or less active than might be expected. Figure 7.5 compares PET scans from two patients: a healthy control (far left) and an AIDS patient (center and far right). The scan illustrates that treatment with AZT significantly affected brain activity in the AIDS patient. As is shown, the AIDS brain without treatment (center) is less active than during treatment (right).

Use What You Know

One of the great gifts that counselors possess is the ability to assess and determine at a deep level the thought processes and emotional responses of their clients—through empathy, active listening, and perhaps even the intangible quality of truly connecting with and accurately understanding other human beings' stories, messages, and meanings. Such is the field you have chosen or that has chosen you—or both. That being said, we encourage counselors to conceptualize cases, assess client brain functioning, and hypothesize about the possible parts of the brain that may be over- or underactive. Though the use of formal assessment tools and brain imaging technologies are of tremendous value and such data can serve to clearly pinpoint brain structural and/or chemical issues, we suggest that your existing skills will be of great value in such assessment as well.

Conclusion

It appears to us that in the years and decades to come, the utility of assessments, especially brain imaging techniques, will continue to grow by leaps and bounds. With each new tool, we will have the opportunity to further assess and investigate the brain in real time as individuals experience different sets of stimuli. Over time, perhaps data sets will be built that truly define the exact science of the connection between brain function and psychological/life issues. Until then, we believe in the utility of not only the current means of assessment but also the skills and talents of professional counselors who utilize their existing skills to better understand the client through a more thorough and clear awareness of the brain and its many functioning parts/activities.

Chapter Review Questions

1. Name and describe three instruments/techniques utilized to assess brain function in clients.
2. Consider and articulate the significant differences found between assessment techniques that utilize imaging versus those that use tests and assessments.
3. Describe the utility of and process involved in an MSE.

8

BRAIN ACTIVITY IN ACTION

As with *any* set of counselor/client responses, there are a multi-tude of differing possibilities. Such is the process of counseling, always in flux and always fluid. We ask that you not get too mired in the rightness or wrongness of the counselor's response, but rather recognize the possibilities that emerge when considering the neurobiological aspects to the interactions.

Case of Sue

Counselor: So what brings you here today, Sue?

Sue: I have been really down lately. I guess it started when Fred and I broke up.

Counselor: I understand that Fred was your longtime boyfriend.

Sue: Yeah, he was. I just (*starts to cry*), I wish things would have turned out different.

Decision point: What parts of the brain would the client access if discussion continued around the emotional aspects of the loss?

Temporal Lobe

What parts of the brain might be accessed if the counselor asks the client to consider what has been learned through the process?

Frontal Lobe

Here we can recognize that from the very start of the session, the counselor's decisions in what to follow up on and what direction to ask the client to go have a profound impact on the parts of the brain that are accessed.

Let us suppose that the counselor uses the latter response.

Counselor: So I can certainly sense and feel your emotion and energy here. I wonder, though, what have you learned from this relationship?

Sue: Well, I guess I learned how bad it hurts when someone you love leaves you for another person. I learned how deep pain can really be.

Now, at this point, the counselor could be aware of the fact that the client is demonstrating true affect (deep feelings), and the part of her brain that is firing the most is probably her *temporal lobe.*

So, what now?

The counselor could choose to stay with the emotions or try to move the client into another part of her brain that may be currently being underutilized (not firing).

Let us say the counselor chooses the latter.

Counselor: I can see that as you talk about him, you are clenching your hands very tightly. Can you tell me a little about what you feel in your hands and forearms as you make those fists?

Sue: I didn't even realize I was doing that. I guess I feel my fingernails digging into my hands, my hands feel moist. I don't really feel anything in my forearms.

Counselor: This is going to be a strange request, but you used the word digging. Can you go through the motion of digging?

Sue: I guess . . . (*She then moves her hands and arms as if using a small shovel to dig.*)

So now, just a few minutes into this session, the counselor has used techniques and process to try to help the client move from some degree of stuckness in her temporal lobe, to her frontal lobe (which did not work immediately), to her parietal lobe (associated with sensing stimuli and motor behavior). What now?

Counselor: Of course, digging can mean many different things to different people. I wonder what this motion and the idea of digging means to you?

Sue: Well, I don't know if this is what you want me to talk about, but I had a really bad relationship with my mother. You know . . . I guess maybe I am digging a hole—you know I used to say things to her when I was a teen that she would always say, "Sue . . . keep it up . . . you're digging yourself into another hole!" I hated when she said that.

So, now the counselor has tried again to access other brain structures, but the client continues back to the temporal lobe—at this point she is tapping into memories. The counselor has, however, helped her to move if only for a moment into the parietal lobe. And, of course, any counselor can recognize that there are a multitude of different directions to go therapeutically.

Counselor: So, now we have talked about the loss of your relationship with Fred and what appear to possibly be some unresolved feelings with your mother. Am I correct?

Sue: Yeah. I guess I don't think much about mom, but yeah, there's a lot there for sure.

Counselor: Loss or meaningful relationships are a theme in your life.

Sue: (*begins to cry—nodding affirmatively*) For sure.

Decision point: Should the counselor go deeper or stay on the surface? Should the counselor address the pain and emotion or move the client into a more cognitive state? Should the counselor work on the past, address the present, or focus the client on the future? There are many decisions here. It appears that the client is in a very emotional (temporal lobe) state of mind. It may be effective to have the client stay there and utilize the strength of one hemisphere over the other. But which one? Left involves logic; right includes imagination and creativity. Our counselor decides to try the right hemisphere.

Counselor: There are some real feelings you have about your mother. It seems as though there is still some stuff there that you never resolved.

Sue: Oh yeah. Lots.

Counselor: I know this might sound strange, but perhaps we could try something. Are you willing to be a bit creative here today?

Sue: Sure.

Counselor: Take a few minutes and draw a picture of your mother and you when you were a teenager.

Sue: Ugh! Ok. Let me think a bit.

Sue then proceeds to draw her mother and herself. Of course, the counselor and client can then address the relationship (through accessing the right hemisphere), loss of relationship, and associated thoughts and feelings. However, it should be noted that moving the client into the right hemisphere might, in this case, allow for a freer process of working on issues and problems the client has around loss without getting stuck in the temporal lobe.

Case of Joe

Counselor: Hi Joe. Where would you like to start today?

Joe: Hey. I guess maybe we should talk some more about my mood swings. This week was pretty bad.

Counselor: OK, so it sounds like you had some real ups and downs this last week.

Joe: Yeah. I know that the meds are supposed to kick in, but right now I feel like they are just making me feel sick and making my emotions even tougher to control.

Counselor: OK, so you are on 10 mg of citalopram—right?

Joe: Yeah, I was on 5 mg a few weeks ago, but the doctor doubled it because it wasn't doing anything for my anxiety.

Counselor: So, I can gather that you have noticed a real difference going from 5 to 10 mg. What are the most significant differences you have found between the two?

Joe: On 5 mg, I didn't feel like there was any difference. Now, on 10, I guess I feel like sometimes I feel like I am super happy, then others, I feel even more nervous and worried.

Discussion: At this point in the session, the counselor has several key choices to make. The counselor can discuss the medications, side effects, issues with changing dosage, and other possible medications that could be considered. Another direction could be for the counselor to assess and work with the good and bad of the highs and lows.

Let us imagine that the counselor goes the route of the former (addressing the medications) first and then addresses the latter.

Counselor: I know that you were just to your doctor for a medication check and that she changed the dosage from 5 to 10, but I want to share with you that there are other medications that can have a positive impact on anxiety. Have you considered talking again to your doctor about other medications?

Joe: I guess. I mean, she knows a lot about meds and said that most people find that this medication works well for anxiety.

Counselor: That may be true that many people respond well. And, you should consider staying open to the fact that it may take some more time for the medication to really start to work fully with your system. But, not all people respond the same to medications. When doctors prescribe, they are typically trying to assess and then pick the best-fit medication. . . . It is not really as exact of a science as we might want to think.

Joe: Hmmmm. I guess I was kinda thinking that maybe it should have worked by now. I think I will call her.

Discussion: Now, the counselor has introduced the idea to the client that he can further advocate for his needs with his prescribing doctor. But the session can continue with the counselor working with what already has been said by the client along with the counselor's awareness of the brain.

Counselor: OK Joe, you said you had some ups and downs. . . . Tell me more about your positive thoughts this week.

Joe: I guess, overall, I mean, I really was less anxious overall. I just realized a few times that I wasn't worrying about anything.

Counselor: OK, so that sounds like you really did have some changes. As you noticed you were not worrying, you felt better about yourself and happier.

Joe: Absolutely! I just felt normal, you know. Like yesterday, I was at work and my boss came in and said we needed to get the tickets filled by the end of the day. In the past,

I would have thought something like, well, I guess the boss is saying I haven't done my job as well as I should have. But yesterday, I just started talking to him and we decided a good way to get the tickets filled. It was pretty cool.

Counselor: I hear pride in what you just said.

Joe: Yeah. Pride. Yeah . . . like I can feel OK even when things around me aren't perfect. But the pride part is that I didn't beat myself up. Maybe the meds are working (*laughs*).

Discussion: In this brief part of a session, the counselor has worked with two distinct parts of the neurocounseling process. The counselor helped the client consider self-advocacy regarding medications and worked on the actual brain structure of the client. Through highlighting and amplifying the positives, the counselor is accessing the frontal lobe.

Case of Ali

Counselor: Hi Ali, where do we want to begin?

Ali: Well, I know this is going to sound weird, but I have been having dreams lately about my dad.

Counselor: It sounds like these dreams about your dad are new and that you are uncertain why you are having them.

Ali: Exactly. I mean, we had a bad relationship and all, but I got over that a long time ago.

Counselor: Bad relationship?

Ali: Well, yeah (*hesitantly*), I mean, he used to hit my mom and brothers and sisters.

Counselor: Oh my, and he hit you also?

Ali: Yeah.

Discussion: At this point, though tough to tell from the dialogue itself, the counselor is experiencing a strong reaction to what the client is discussing. The client is describing abuse at the hands of her father; the counselor had a similar experience in her childhood—and has not fully worked through her abuse.

Although the similarity in their stories can be useful in the counselor's empathy, the overall story of the client brings on strong and immediate reactions by the counselor. The session continues.

Counselor: I can only imagine that you must still hate him at some level.

Ali: Well, I guess, I mean, I don't hate him all the time, I just feel like I wish we could have been closer.

Counselor: Sure, but there are some things that cannot be taken back or changed (*in the counselor's mind, the trauma of abuse is flashing*).

At this point in the session, the counselor has had her PTSD triggered and is stuck in the right hemisphere. Because the corpus callosum is smaller and not allowing for clear communication between the right and left hemisphere, there is little chance of the counselor moving into a more logic-oriented mind-set—which of course significantly diminishes the possibility of true therapy to occur.

Case of Tim

Counselor: Hi Tim.

Tim: Hello.

Counselor: Where would you like to start?

Tim: I guess, I have been thinking about how mad I get at my roommate for not including me in what they all do. You know, like, we are all outcasts anyhow, but I am the outcast of the group. I would say something to him, but he already has low self-esteem, and I would cause him even more harm.

Counselor: OK, I can feel a lot of energy around this topic, and it sounds like you are feeling both frustrated and upset about being left out.

Tim: Yeah, exactly. I mean, it's not that big of a deal, but I am trying to find a way to let him know without hurting him.

At this point in the session, the counselor can sense a lot of emotion about the topic but also can tell that the client has done a lot of thinking about this problem lately. The counselor decides that the client's frontal and temporal lobes are very active. She decides to try to move the client more fully into the parietal lobe and cerebellum.

Counselor: Tim, I wonder if we can try something creative here . . . OK?

Tim: Sure.

Counselor: I want you to think about the major groups of which you are a member. You mentioned being a member of the outcasts. Think of a few other groups, and then we will begin.

The counselor has just reassigned a task to the client's frontal lobe. She asked him to stop thinking about the problem and tackle the assignment of logically assigning value to several other groups of which he is a member.

Counselor: (*after a few moments, when it appears Tim has decided on a few more groups*) OK, so now, on this paper, using whatever colors you want, let's be creative.

Tim: (*Smiles.*) OK.

Counselor: Use your imagination and create in any way you want, symbolically, the groups you are a member of.

Tim: OK. (*He then proceeds to draw out three different groups/ symbols.*)

Counselor: OK, now, take some time and pick out a few words or phrases that best reflect these groups' best advice for you to handle this issue with your roommate.

Tim: Oh, OK, I see.

> The counselor has now assigned a motor-based task that more fully balances the client's psychic energy on the problem. Through imagery and the empowerment of other voices, the client is tasked with problem solving (through the frontal lobe) in a way that he was not previously able to access.

Conclusion

Inherent in the process of neurocounseling is the aptitude of the counselor to recognize the possible client brain function as the process of therapy unfolds. Through practice and considered value of the basic and advanced aspects of neurobiology offered in this chapter and throughout this book, counselors are armed with yet another highly effective and efficient way to help clients cope with (overcome, etc.) their personal psychological distress. In years to come, of course, there will be many more research studies and clinical understandings of the brain that will further aid us all in the noble and critical work we do.

REFERENCES

Alenina, N., Bashammakh, S., & Bader, M. (2006). Specifications and differentiation of serotonergic neurons. *Stem Cell Reviews, 2,* 5–10.

Alexander, A.L., Lee, J.E., Lazar, M., Boudos, R., et al. (2007). Diffusion tensor imaging of the corpus callosum in autism. *Neuroimage, 34,* 61–73.

Allen, G. (2005). The cerebellum in autism. *Clinical Neuropsychology, 2,* 321–337.

American Counseling Association. (2005). ACA code of ethics. Retrieved from http://www.counseling.org/Resources/CodeOfEthics/TP/Home/CT2.aspx

American Psychiatric Association. (2000). *Diagnostic and statistical manual of mental disorders* (4th ed., text rev.). Washington, DC: Author.

Andover, M.S., Pepper, C.M., Ryabchenko, K.A., Orrico, E.G., & Gibb, B.E. (2005). Self-mutilation and symptoms of depression, anxiety, and borderline personality disorder. *Suicide and Life-Threatening Behavior, 35*(5), 581–591.

Arakawa, R., Ito, H., Takano, A., Okumura, M., Takahashi, H., Takano, H., Okuba, Y., & Suhura, T. (2010). Dopamine D2 receptor occupancy by perospirone: A positron emission tomography study in patients with schizophrenia and healthy subjects. *Psychopharmacology, 209,* 285–290.

Armstrong, E., Zilles, K., & Schleicher, A. (1993). Cortical folding and the evolution of the human brain. *Journal of Human Evolution, 25,* 387–392.

Bank, P. (2012). Brief overview of common psychotropic medications: A practical guide from a clinical viewpoint. Retrieved from http://ssw.umich.edu/public/currentprojects/icwtp/mentalhealth/Brief_Overview_of_Common_Psychotropic_Medications.pdf

Barlow, D.H. (2002). *Anxiety and its disorders: The nature and treatment of anxiety and panic* (2nd ed.). New York: Guilford Press.

Beeman, M.J., & Bowden, E.M. (2000). The right hemisphere maintains solution-related activation for yet-to-be solved insight problems. *Memory & Cognition, 28,* 1231–1241.

Begley, S. (2007). *Train your mind, change your brain: How a new science reveals our extraordinary potential to transform ourselves.* New York: Random House.

Black, J.E., Isaacs, K.R., Anderson, B.J., Alcantara, A.A., & Greenough, W.T. (1990). Learning causes synaptogenesis, whereas motor activity causes angiogenesis, in cerebellar cortex of adult rats (paramedian lobule/neural plasticity/exercise). *Neurobiology, 87,* 5568–5572.

Blumenfeld, H. 2002. *Neuroanatomy through clinical cases.* Sunderland, MA: Sinauer Associates.

Bremner, J.D. (2002). *Does stress damage the brain?* New York: Norton.

Bremner, J.D. (2006). Traumatic stress: Effects on the brain. *Dialogues in Clinical Neuroscience, 8*(4).

Brezun, J.M., & Daszuta, A. (2000). Serotonin may stimulate granule cell proliferation in the adult hippocampus, as observed in rats grafted with foetal raphe neurons. *European Journal of Neuroscience, 21,* 391–396.

Brooks, F., & McHenry, B. (2009). *A contemporary approach to substance abuse and addiction counseling.* Alexandria, VA: American Counseling Association.

Bunge, S.A., Hazeltine, E., Scanlon, M.D., Rosen, A.D., & Gabrieli, J.D.E. (2002). Dissociable contributions of prefrontal and parietal cortices to response selection. *Neuroimage, 17,* 1562–1571.

Cade, B., & O'Hanlon, W.H. (1999). *A brief guide to brief therapy.* New York: Norton.

Casanova, M.F., El-Baz, A., Mott, M., Mannheim, G., Hasan, H., Fahmi, R., et al. (2009). Reduced gyral window and corpus callosum size in autism: Possible macroscopic correlates of a minicolumnopathy. *Journal of Autism and Developmental Disorders, 39,* 751–764.

Centonze, D., Rossi, S., Prosperetti, C., Tscherter, A., Bernardi, G., Maccarrone, M., & Calabresi, P. (2005). Abnormal sensitivity to cannabinoid receptor stimulation might contribute to altered gamma-aminobutyric acid transmission in the striatum of R6/2 Huntington's disease mice. *Biological Psychiatry, 57,* 1583–1589.

Champagne, F.A., Chretien, P., Stevenson, C.W., Zhang, T.Y., Gratton, A., & Meaney, M.J. (2004). Variations in nucleus accumbens dopamine associated with individual differences in maternal behavior in the rat. *The Journal of Neuroscience, 24,* 4113–4123.

Chance, P. (2009). *Learning and Behavior.* Belmont, CA: Wadsworth.

Clark, R.E., Manns, J.R., & Squire, L.R. (2002). Classical conditioning, awareness, and brain systems. *Trends in Cognitive Sciences, 6,* 524–531.

Cohen, R., Swerdlik, M., & Sturman, E. (2013). *Psychological testing and assessment* (8th ed.). New York: McGraw Hill.

Cook-Cottone, C. (2004). Childhood posttraumatic stress disorder: Diagnosis, treatment and school reintegration. *School Psychology Review, 33*(1), 127–139.

Coppen, A. (1967). The biochemistry of affective disorders. *The British Journal of Psychiatry, 113,* 1237–1264.

Corey, G. (2009). *Theory and practice of counseling and psychotherapy.* Belmont, CA: Brooks Cole.

Creeden, K. (2009). How trauma and attachment can impact neurodevelopment: Informing our understanding and treatment of sexual behavior problems. *Journal of Sexual Aggression, 15*(3), 261–273.

De Bellis, M., Keshavan, M., Clark, D., Casey, B., Giedd, J., Boring, A., Frustaci, K., & Ryan, N. (1999). Developmental traumatology part II: Brain development. *Society of Biological Psychiatry, 45,* 1271–1284.

De Bellis, M.D., Keshevan, M.S., Shifflett, H., Iyengar, S., Beers, S.R., Hall, J., & Moritz, G. (2002). Brain structures in pediatric maltreatment-related posttraumatic stress disorder: A sociodemograpically matched study. *Biological Psychiatry, 52,* 1066.

de Bruin, J., Swinkels, W., & de Brabander, J. (1997). Response learning of rats in a Morris water maze: Involvement of the medial prefrontal cortex. *Behavioural Brain Research, 85,* 47–51.

De Carolis, L., Stasi, M.A., Serlupi-Crescenzi, O., Borsini, F., & Nencini, P. (2010). The effects of clozapine on quinpirole-induced non-regulatory drinking and prepulse inhibition disruption in rats. *Psychopharmacology, 212,* 105–115.

De Lange, F.P., Koers, A., Kalkman, J.S., Bleijenberg, G., Hagoort, P., et al. (2008). Increase in prefrontal cortical volume following cognitive behavioral therapy in patients with chronic fatigue syndrome. *Brain, 131,* 2172–2180.

De Robertis, E.D.P., & Bennett, H.S. (1955). *Journal of Biophys Biochem Cytol, 1,* 47–58.

Depraz, N., Varela, F., & Vermersch, P. (2003). *On becoming aware.* Philadelphia: John Benjamins.

Dodd, M.L., Klos, K.J., Bower, J.H., Geda, Y.E., Josephs, K.A., et al. (2005). Pathological gambling caused by drugs used to treat Parkinson disease. *Arch Neurol, 62,* 1377–1381.

Drummond, R.J., & Jones, K.D. (2010). *Assessment procedures for counselors and helping professionals* (7th ed.). Upper Saddle River, NJ: Pearson/Merrill Prentice Hall.

Ellis, A. (2001). *Overcoming destructive beliefs, feelings and behaviors: New directions for rational emotive behavioral therapy.* New York: Prometheus Books.

Emick, J., & Welsh, M.C. (2005). Association between formal operational thought and executive functions. *Learning and Individual Differences, 15,* 177–188.

Erikson, E. (1980). *Identity and the life cycle.* New York: Norton.

Ernst, M. (1997). Studies of brain structure and brain activity in children with attention deficit disorders. In G.R. Lyon & J. Rumsey (Eds.),

Neuroimaging: A window to the neurological foundations of learning and behavior. Baltimore: Paul H. Brookes.

Ernst, M., Bolla, K., Mouratidis, M., Contoreggi, C., Matochik, J.A., Kurian, V., Cadet, J.L., Kimes, A.S., & London, E.D. (2002). Decision-making in a risk-taking task: A PET study. *Neuropsychopharmacology, 26,* 682–691.

Ernst, M., Cohen, R.M., Liebenauer, L.L., Johns, P.H., & Zametkin, A.J. (1997). Cerebral glucose metabolism in adolescent girls with attention deficit/hyperactivity disorder. *Journal of the American Academy of Child and Adolescent Psychiatry, 36,* 1399–1406.

Ernst, M., Liebenauer, L.L., King, A.C., Fitzgerald, G.A., Cohen, R.M., & Zametkin, A.J. (1994). Reduced brain metabolism in hyperactive girls. *Journal of the American Academy of Child & Adolescent Psychiatry, 33,* 858–868.

Fairless, R., Masius, H., Rohlmann, A., Heupel, K., Ahmad, M., Reissner, C., Dresbach, T., & Missler, M. (2008). Polarized targeting of neurexins to synapses is regulated by their C-terminal sequences. *Journal of Neuroscience, 28*(48).

Fatemi, S., Aldinger, K., Ashwood, P., Bauman, M., Blaha, C., et al. (2012). Consensus paper: Pathological role of the cerebellum in autism. *The Cerebellum,* 1–31.

Favazza, A.R., DeRosear, L., & Conterio, K. (1989). Self-mutilation and eating disorders. *Suicide and Life-Threatening Behaviors, 19,* 352–361.

Ferguson, J.M. (2001). SSRI antidepressant medications: adverse effects and tolerability. *Primary Care Companion to the Journal of Clinical Psychiatry, 3,* 22.

Ferguson, J.N., Aldag, J.M., Insel, T.R., & Young, L.J. (2001). Oxytocin in the medial amygdala is essential for social recognition in the mouse. *The Journal of Neuroscience, 21*(20).

Francis, D.D., Champagne, F.C., & Meaney, M.J. (2000). Variations in maternal behaviour are associated with differences in oxytocin receptor levels in the rat. *Journal of Neuroendocrinol, 12,* 1145–1148.

Frazier, T., Barnea-Goraly, N., & Hardan, A. (2010). Evidence for anatomical alterations in the corpus callosum in autism spectrum disorders. *European Psychiatric Review, 3*(2), 29–33.

Frazier, T., Keshavan, M., Minshew, N., & Hardan, A. (2012). A two-year longitudinal MRI study of the corpus callosum in autism. *Journal of Autism and Developmental Disorders, 42*(11), 2312–2322.

Garland, E.L., & Howard, M.O. (2009). Neuroplasticity, psychosocial genomics, and the biopsychosocial paradigm in the 21st century. *Health and Social Work, 34,* 191–199.

Gimpl, G., & Fahrenholz, F. (2001). The oxytocin receptor system: Structure, function and regulation. *Physiological Reviews, 81,* 629–683.

Gladding, S. (2001). *Counseling: A comprehensive profession* (6th ed.). Upper Saddle River, NJ: Pearson.

Goldapple, K., Segal, Z., Garson, C., Lau, M., Bieling, P., Kennedy, S., et al. (2004). Modulation of cortical-limbic pathways in major depression: Treatment-specific effects of cognitive behavior therapy. *Archives of General Psychology, 61,* 34–41.

Goldschmidt, H., & Roelke, D. (2012). Dreams and the unconscious through the lens of neuro-psychoanalysis: A look at unconscious motivational systems within the brain. *Center for Psychotherapy and Psychoanalysis of New Jersey.*

Gregory, R. (1999). *Foundations of intellectual assessment.* Needham Heights, MA: Allyn & Bacon.

Grey, E. (2010). Use your brain: A neurobiologically driven application of REBT with children. *Journal of Creativity in Mental Health, 5,* 55–64.

Hammond, C. (2008). *Cellular and molecular neurophysiology* (3rd ed.). Burlington, MA: Academic Press.

Harper, H., Rodwell, V., & Mayes, P. (1977). *Review of physiological chemistry* (16th ed.). Los Altos, CA: Lange Medical Publications.

Henderson, D., & Thompson, C. (2011). *Counseling children* (8th ed.). Belmont, CA: Cengage.

Herculano-Houzel, S. (2009). The human brain in numbers: A lineal scaled-up primate brain. *Human Neuroscience, 3*(31).

Herman, B.H., Hammock, K.M., Arthur-Smith, A., Egan, J., Chatoor, I., Werner, A., & Zelnick, N. (2004). Naltrexone decreases self-injurious behavior. *Annals of Neurology, 22,* 520–522.

Hood, A., & Johnson, R.W. (2007). *Assessment in counseling: A guide to the use of psychological assessment procedures* (4th ed.). Alexandria, VA: American Counseling Association.

Iaccino, J. (1993). *Left brain–right brain differences: Inquiries, evidence, and new approaches.* Hillsdale, NJ: Lawrence Earlbaum Associates, Inc.

Ivey, A., & Ivey, M.B. (2003). *Intentional interviewing and counseling* (5th ed.). Belmont, CA: Brooks Cole.

Jackowski, A., de Araújo, C., de Lacerda, A., de Jesus Mari, J., & Kaufman, J. (2009). Neurostructural imaging findings in children with post-traumatic stress disorder: Brief review. *Psychiatry & Clinical Neurosciences, 63*(1), 1–8. doi:10.1111/j.1440–1819.2008.01906.x.

Jung-Beeman, M., Bowden, E.M., Haberman, J., Frymiare, J.L., Arambel-Liu, S., Greenblatt, R., Reber, P.J., & Kounios, J. (2004). Neural activity when people solve verbal problems with insight. PLoS Biol 2(4): e97. doi:10.1371/journal.pbio.0020097

Just, M.A., Cherkassky, V.L., Keller, T.A., & Minshew, N.J. (2004). Cortical activation and synchronization during sentence comprehension in high-functioning autism: Evidence of underconnectivity. *Department of Psychology, paper 323.* Retrieved from http://repository.cmu.edu/psychology/323

Kaas, R., Goovaerts, M.J., Dhaene, J., & Denuit, M. (2008). *Modern actuarial risk theory: Using R.* New York: Springer.

Kandel, E. (2000). *Principles of neural science.* New York: McGraw Hill.

Kandel, E.R. (1998). A new intellectual framework for psychiatry. *American Journal of Psychiatry, 155,* 457–469.

Kanner, L. (1943). Autistic disturbances of affective contact. *Nervous Child, 2,* 217–250.

Kars, H., Broekema, W., Glaudemans-van Geldern, I., Verhoeven, W.M.A., & van Ree, J.M. (1990). Naltrexone attenuates self-injurious behavior in mentally retarded subjects. *Biological Psychiatry, 27,* 741–746.

Katz, D., & Steinmetz, J. (2002). Psychological functions of the cerebellum. *Behavioral Cognitive Neuroscience Reviews, 1*(3), 229–241.

Kay, J. (2009). Toward a neurobiology of child psychotherapy. *Journal of Loss and Trauma, 14,* 287–303.

Kempermann, G. (2011). Seven principles in the regulation of adult neurogenesis. *European Journal of Neuroscience, 33,* 1018–1024.

Kempermann, G., Gast, D., Kronenberg, G., Yamaguchi, M., & Gage, F.H. (2003). Early determination and long-term persistence in adult-generated new neurons in the hippocampus of mice. *Development, 130,* 391–399.

Kennedy, S., Konarski, J.Z., Segal, Z.V., Lau, M.A., Bieling, P.J., McIntyre, R.S., et al. (2007). Differences in brain glucose metabolism between responders to CBT and venlafaxine in a 16-week controlled trial. *American Journal of Psychiatry, 165,* 778–788.

Kerr, A.L., Steuer, E.L., Pochtarev, V., & Swain, R.A. (2010). Angiogenesis but not neurogenesis is critical for normal learning and memory acquisition. *Neuroscience, 24,* 214–226.

Kerr, A.L., & Swain, R.A. (2011). Rapid cellular genesis and apoptosis: Effects of exercise in the adult rat. *Behavioral Neuroscience, 125,* 1–9.

King-Casas, B., Tomlin, D., Anen, C., Camerer, C.F., Quartz, S.R., & Montague, R. (2005). Getting to know you: Reputation and trust in a two-person economic exchange. *Science, 308,* 78–83.

Kjernisted, K. (2006). Causes and cures: The neurobiology of symptoms and treatment in anxiety disorders. *Canadian Journal of Psychiatry, 51,* 5.

Knapp, M.L., & Vangelisti, A.L. (2000). *Interpersonal communication and human relationships* (4th ed.). Boston: Allyn & Bacon.

Kolb, B., & Whishaw, I. (2010). *Fundamentals of human neuropsychology.* New York: Worth Publishers.

Kounios, J., & Beeman, M. (2010). The aha! moment: The cognitive neuroscience of insight. *Current Directions in Psychological Science, 18,* 210–216.

Krueger, F., McCabe, K., Moll, J., Kriegeskorte, N., Zahn, R., Strenziok, M., Heinecke, A., & Grafman, J. (2007). Neural correlates of trust. *PNAS, 104*(50).

Kuhn, R. (1958). The treatment of depressive states with G 22355 (imipramine hydrochloride). *American Journal of Psychiatry, 115,* 459–464.

Lambert, M.J., & Ogles, B.M. (2004). The efficacy and effectiveness of psychotherapy. In M.J. Lambert (Ed.), *Bergin and Garfield's handbook of psychotherapy and behavior change* (5th ed., pp. 139–193). New York: Wiley.

Landreth, G. (2012). *Play therapy* (3rd ed.). New York: Routledge.

Liberman, M. (2009). *Putting feelings into words.* Lecture at the Association for the Advancement of Science. Chicago, IL (2009, February).

Linden, D. (2006). How psychotherapy changes the brain—The contribution of functional imaging. *Molecular Psychiatry, 11,* 538–538.

Liu, D., Diorio, J., Tannenbaum, B., Caldji, C., Francis, D., Freedman, A., et al. (1997). Maternal care, hippocampal glucocorticoid receptors, and hypothalamic-pituitary-adrenal responses to stress. *Science, 277*(5332), 1659–1662.

Lopez-Munoz, F., Boya, J., & Alamo, C. (2006). Neuron theory, the cornerstone of neuroscience, on the centenary of the Nobel Prize award to Santiago Ramon y Cajal. *Brain Research Bulletin, 70,* 391–405.

Lou, H.C., Henriksen, L., & Bruhn, P. (1990). Focal cerebral dysfunction in developmental learning disabilities. *The Lancet, 335,* 8–11.

Lou, H.C., Henriksen, L., Bruhn, P., et al. (1984). Focal cerebral hypoperfusion in children with dysphasia and/or attention deficit disorder. *Archives of Neurology, 41,* 825–829.

Lou, H.C., Henriksen, L., Bruhn, P., et al. (1989). Striatal dysfunction in attention deficit hyperkinetic disorder. *Archives of Neurology, 46,* 48–52.

Luders, E., Thompson, P.M., & Toga, A.W. (2010). The development of the corpus callosum. *Journal of Neuroscience, 30,* 10985–10990.

Lutz, A., Greischar, L.L., Rawlings, N.B., Ricard, M., & Davidson, R.J. (2004). Long-term meditators self-induce high-amplitude gamma synchrony during mental practice. *Proceedings in the National Academy of Science 01*(46), 16369–16373.

Maguire, E.A., Gadian, D.G., Johnsrude, I.S., Good, C.D., Ashburner, J., Frackowiak, R.S.J., & Frith, C.D. (2000). Navigation-related structural change in the hippocampi of taxi drivers. *PNAS, 97,* 4398–4403.

Martin, S.D., Martin, E., Rai, S.S., Richardson, M.A., Royall, R., & Eng, C. (2001). Brain blood flow changes in depressed patients treated with interpersonal psychotherapy or venlafaxine hydrochloride: Preliminary findings. *Archives of General Psychiatry, 58,* 641.

McAlonan, G.M., Cheung, V., Cheung, C., Suckling, J., Lam, G.Y., Tai, K.S., Yip, L., et al. (2005). Mapping the brain in autism. A voxel-based MRI study of volumetric differences and intercorrelations in autism. *Brain, 28*(2), 268–276.

McEwen, B. (2000). The neurobiology of stress: From serendipity to clinical relevance. *Brain Resolution, 886,* 172–189.

McGaugh, J.L. (2000). Memory—A century of consolidation. *Science, 287,* 248–251.

McHenry, B., & McHenry, J. (2006). *What therapists say and why they say it.* Boston: Pearson.

Meerabux, J., Iwayama, Y., Sakurai, T., Ohba, H., Toyota, T., et al. (2005). Association of an orexin 1 receptor 408Val variant with polydipsia-hyponatremia in schizophrenic subjects. *Biological Psychiatry, 58,* 401–407.

Moore, R.Y., & Halaris, A.E. (1975). Hippocampal innervation by serotonin neurons of the midbrain raphe in the rat. *The Journal of Comparative Neurology, 164,* 171–183.

Morgan, M.A., Romanski, L.M., & LeDoux, J.E. (1993). Extinction of emotional learning: Contribution of medial prefrontal cortex. *Neuroscience Letters,* 163, 109–113.

Murdock, N. (2012). *Theories of counseling and psychotherapy: A case approach* (3rd ed.). Boston: Pearson.

Nelson, J.C., Mazure, C.M., Jatlow, P.I., Bowers Jr., M.B, & Price, L.H. (1997). Combining norepinephrine and serotonin reuptake inhibition mechanisms for treatment of depression: A double-blind, randomized study. *Biological Psychiatry, 55,* 296–300.

Newman, J.D. (2007). Neural circuits underlying crying and cry responding in mammals. *Behavioral Brain Research, 182,* 155–165.

Nishijima, T., Okamoto, M., Matsui, T., Kita, I., & Soya, H. (2012). Hippocampal functional hyperemia mediated by NMDA receptor/NO signaling in rats during mild exercise. *Applied Physiology, 112*(1), 197–203.

Nishijima, T., & Soya, H. (2006). Evidence of functional hyperemia in the rat hippocampus during mild treadmill running. *Neuroscience Research, 54,* 186–191.

Numan, M., & Sheehan, T.P. (1997).Neuroanatomical circuitry for mammalian maternal behavior. *Annals of the New York Academy of Sciences, 807.*

O'Halloran, C.J., Kinsella, G.J., & Storey, E. (2011). The cerebellum and neuropsychological functioning: A critical review. *Journal of Clinical and Experiential Neuropsychology, 34*(1), 35–56.

Palade, G.E., & Palay, S.L. (1954). Electron microscope observations of interneuronal and neuromuscular synapses. *Anatomical Record, 118,* 335.

Parihar, V.K., Hattiangady, B., Kuruba, R., Shual, B., & Shetty, A.K. (2011). Predictable chronic mild stress improves mood, hippocampal neurogenesis and memory. *Molecular Psychiatry, 16,* 171–183.

Pascual-Leone, A., Amedi, A., Fegni, F., & Merabet, L.B. (2005). The plastic human brain cortex. *Annual Reviews of Neuroscience, 28,* 377–401.

Perry, B. (2001). The neurodevelopmental impact of violence in childhood. In D. Schetky & E. Benedek (Eds.), *Textbook of child and adolescent forensic psychiatry* (pp. 231–238). Washington, DC: American Psychiatric Press.

Perry, B.D. (2009). Examining child maltreatment through a neurodevelopmental lens: Clinical applications of the neurosequential model of therapeutics. *Journal of Loss and Trauma, 14,* 240–255.

Piven, J., Bailey, J., Ranson, B., & Arndt, S. (1997). An MRI study of the corpus callosum in autism. *American Journal of Psychiatry, 154*, 1051–1056.

Pons, T., Garraghty, P.E., Ommaya, A.K., Kaas, J.H., Taub, E., & Mishkin, M. (1991). Massive cortical reorganization after sensory deafferentation in adult macaques. *Science, 252*, 1857–1860.

Ramon y Cajal, S. (1917). *Recuerdos de mi vida.* Spain: Madrid Imprenta y Librería de N. Spain.

Rao, H., Korczykowski, M., Pluta, J., Houng, A., & Detre, J.A. (2008). Neural correlates of voluntary and involuntary risk taking in the human brain: An fMRI study of the balloon analog risk task (BART). *Neuroimage, 42*, 902–910.

Reuter, J., Raedler, T., Rose, M., Hand, I., Glascher, J., et al. (2005). Pathological gambling is linked to reduced activation of the mesolimbic reward system. *Nature Neuroscience, 8*, 147–148.

Rogers, C. (1951). *Client-centered therapy.* London: Constable.

Rossi, E.L. (2005). The ideodynamic action hypothesis of therapeutic suggestion: Creative replay in the psychosocial genomics of therapeutic hypnosis. *European Journal of Clinical Hypnosis, 6*(2), 2–12.

Rossoni, E., Feng, J., Tirozzi, B., Brown, D., Leng, G., & Moos, F. (2008). Emergent synchronous bursting of oxytocin neuronal network. *PLoS: Computational Biology, 4*, e1000123. doi:10.1371/journal.pcbi.1000123.

Rubin, J., & Terman, D. (2012). Explicit maps to predict activation order in multiphase rhythms of a coupled cell network. *The Journal of Mathematical Neuroscience, 2*(4).

Sahay, A., & Hen, R. (2007). Adult hippocampal neurogenesis in depression. *Nature Neuroscience, 10*, 1110–1115.

Scheele, D., Striepens, N., Gunturkun, O., Deutschlander, S., Maier, W., Kendrick, K.M., & Hurlman, R. (2012). Oxytocin modulates social distance between males and females. *Journal of Neuroscience, 32*, 16074–16079.

Schneiderman, I., Zagoory-Sharon, O., Leckman, J.F., & Feldman, R. (2012). Oxytocin during the initial stages of romantic attachment: Relations to couples' interactive reciprocity. *Psychoneuroendocrinology, 37*, 1277–1285.

Schwartz, J.M., & Begley, S. (2002). *The mind and the brain: Neuroplasticity and the power of the mental force.* New York: Harper Collins.

Seigel, D. (2007). *The mindful brain.* New York: W.W. Norton.

Shedler, J. (2010). The efficacy of psychodynamic psychotherapy. *American Psychologist, 65*(2).

Shin, L.M., Orr, S.P., Carson, M.A., Rausch, S.L, Macklin, M.L., Lasko, N.B., & Pitman, R.K. (2004). Regional cerebral blood flow in the amygdala and medial prefrontal cortex during traumatic imagery in male and female Vietnam patients with PTSD. *Archives of General Psychiatry, 61*, 168.

Shin, L.M., Rauch, S.R., & Pitman, R.K. (2006). Amygdala, medial prefrontal cortex, and hippocampal function in PTSD. *Annals of the New York Academy of Sciences, 1071*, 67–79.

Sikorski, A.M., Price, K., Morton, G., Duran, J., Cool, J., Whetmore, B., & Jennings, M. (2012). A *single acute bout of aerobic activity improves memory retention in sedentary, but not physically active, adults.* Manuscript submitted for publication.

Sikorski, A.M., & Swain, R.A. (2006, October). *Angiogenesis inhibition impairs spatial learning in adult rats.* Presented at the 36th Society of Neuroscience Annual Meeting, Atlanta.

Stanley, B., Sher, L., Wilson, S., Ekman, R., Huang, Y., & Mann, J. (2010). Nonsuicidal self-injurious behavior, endogenous opioids and monoamine neurotransmitters. *Journal of Affective Disorders, 124,* 134–140.

Stern, E., & Taylor, S.F. (2009). Topographic analysis of individual activation patterns in medial frontal cortex in schizophrenia. *Human Brain Mapping, 30*(7):2146–2156.

Stern, J.M. & Taylor, J.A. (1991). Haloperidol inhibits maternal retrieval and licking, but enhances nursing behavior and litter weight gains in lactating rats. *Journal of Endocrinology, 3,* 591–596.

Straube, T., Mentzel, H.J., & Miltner, W.H. (2006). Neural mechanisms of automatic and direct processing of phobogenic stimuli in specific phobia. *Biological Psychiatry, 59,* 162–170.

Stuss, D.T. (1992). Biological and psychological development of executive functions. *Brain and Cognition, 20,* 8–23.

Suyemoto, K. (1998). The functions of self-mutilation. *Clinical Psychology Review, 18*(5), 531–554.

Symons, F.J., Thompson, A., & Rodriguez, M.R. (2004). Self-injurious behavior and the efficacy of naltrexone treatment: A quantitative review. *Mental Retardation and Developmental Disabilities Research Reviews, 10,* 193–200.

Szymanski, L., Kedesdy, J., Sulkes, S., Cutier, A., & Stevens-Our, P. (1987). Naltrexone in treatment of self-injurious behavior: A clinical study. *Research on Developmental Disabilities, 8,* 179–190.

Tait, D.S., Brown, V.J., Farovik, A., Theobald, D.E., Dalley, J.W., & Robbins T.W. (2007). Lesions of the dorsal noradrenergic bundle impair attentional set-shifting in the rat. *European Journal of Neuroscience, 25,* 3719–3724. doi: 10.1111/j.1460–9568.2007.05612.x.

Teicher, M.H., Dumont, N.L., Ito, Y., et al. (2004). Childhood neglect is associated with reduced corpus callosum area. *Biological Psychiatry, 56,* 80–85.

van der Kolk, B. (2003). The neurobiology of childhood trauma and abuse. *Child and Adolescent Psychiatry Clinics of North America, 12,* 293–317.

van Praag, H., Christie, B.R., Sejnowski, T.J., & Gage, F.H. (1999a). Running enhances neurogenesis, learning, and long-term potentiation in mice. Proceedings of the National Academy of Science, *96,* 13427–13431.

van Praag, H., Kempermann, G., & Gage, F.H. (1999b). Running increases cell proliferation and neurogenesis in the adult mouse dentate gyrus. *Nature Neuroscience 2*, 266–270.

Villarreal, G., Hamilton, D., Graham, D., Driscoll, I., Qualls, C., Petropoulos, H., & Brooks, W. (2004). Reduced area of the corpus callosum in posttraumatic stress disorder. *Psychiatric Research: Neuroimaging, 131*(3), 227–235.

Wager, T.D., Rilling, J.K., Smith, E.E., Sokolik, A., Casey, K.L., Davidson, R.J., et al. (2004). Placebo-induced changes in fMRI in the anticipation and experience of pain. *Science, 303*(5661), 1162–1167.

White, M., & Epston, D. (1990). *Narrative means to therapeutic ends.* New York: W.W. Norton.

Wiesel, T.N., & Hubel, D.H. (1963). Effects of visual deprivation on morphology and physiology of cells in the cats lateral geniculate nucleus body. *Journal of Neurophysiology, 26*, 987–993.

Willemsen-Swinkels, S., Buitelaar, J.K., Nijhof, G.J., & van Engeland, H. (1995). Failure of naltrexone hydrochloride to reduce self-injurious and autistic behaviour in mentally retarded adults: Double-blinded placebo-controlled studies. *Archives of General Psychiatry, 52*(9), 766–773.

Williams, L.M., Grieve, S.M., Whitford, T.J., Clark, C.R., Gur, R.C., Goldberg, E., et al. (2005). Neural synchrony and gray matter variation in human males and females: Integration of 40 Hz gamma synchrony and MRI measures. *Journal of Integrative Neuroscience, 4*, 77–93.

Worden, J.W. (2002). *Grief counseling and grief therapy* (3rd ed.). New York: Springer Publishing Company.

Zametkin, A., Ernst, M., & Cohen, R. (1999). 9 single gene studies of ADHD. *Attention, Genes and ADHD*, 157.

Zametkin, A.J., Leibenauer, L.L., Fitzgerald, G.A., King, A.C., Minkunas, D.V., Herscovitch, P., & Cohen, R.M. (1993). *Archives of General Psychiatry, 50*, 333.

Zuckerman, E. (2005). *Clinicians thesaurus (6th ed.).* New York: Guilford Press.

INDEX